Archaeology

Michael Carter

Archaeology

BLANDFORD PRESS

Poole   Dorset

First published in the U.K. in 1980.

Copyright © 1980 Blandford Press Ltd,
Link House, West Street,
Poole, Dorset, BH15 1LL

**British Library Cataloguing in
Publication Data**
Carter, Michael
  Archaeology in colour.
  1. Archaeology
  I. Title
  930'.1   CC165

ISBN 0 7137 0861 1 (Hardback edition)
ISBN 0 7137 1067 5 (Paperback edition)

Set in 10/10½ Monophoto Apollo
by Oliver Burridge & Co. Ltd.
Printed in Hong Kong
by South China Printing Co.

Contents

Acknowledgements

The illustrations in this book have mainly come from The Ridley Collection. Particular acknowledgement is, however, due to the following for colour illustrations: Ashmolean Museum, Oxford, 20, 55, 56; Birmingham City Museum, UK, 20, 37, 66, 67; British Museum, 11, 14, 16, 18, 19, 22, 39, 40, 51, 54; Bristol City Museum, 13, 17; Colchester and Essex Museum, 45; Department of the Environment, UK, 52; Freer Gallery, Washington, 63, 64; Heraclion Museum, Crete, 24, 25, 26, 27; National Museum of Anthropology, Mexico, 65; National Museum of Malta, 32, 36; Origination Picture Library, 10, 21, 23, 41, 47, 61, 62; George Rainbird Ltd., (F. L. Kennett), 15; Sotheby's, London, 12.

Further acknowledgement is also due to the following for black and white illustrations: British Museum, pp. 36, 43, 44, 46, 49, 51, 53, 54, 112, 117, 118, 133; Dorset County Museum, p. 132; Heraclion Museum, Crete, p. 58; Museum of Mankind, London, pp. 152, 154; National Museum of Malta, p. 111; Origination Picture Library, p. 12; Russell-Cotes Museum, Bournemouth, p. 16.

7

Foreword

Any account of archaeology must deal with four separate aspects—
what archaeology is; how it works; the archaeologists who made it
work, and how the results of their labours have helped supplement
historical documents.

The early history of archaeology itself is in reality an account of both
the development of archaeological techniques and of the men and
women who invented and developed the techniques; whose intuition,
flair, imagination and learning have led to the discovery and understanding of the major civilizations of the world. Both these factors—
techniques and personalities—have played a major part in the growth
of our knowledge of human history.

In this book, I have begun with an account of the discoverers—the
men and women who found history; and followed this with an examination of the techniques and methods of archaeology of the early days
and descriptions of some of the more sophisticated techniques of today.
The major part of the book consists of a world-wide account of some of
the discoveries and history that archaeologists have helped to write by
unearthing evidence from the ground. Inevitably, in a book of this size,
it has been necessary to be selective in the facts presented and to gener-
alise in others, but the volume makes no scholarly pretences. It is aimed
at giving an account of archaeology as a whole, and how it has helped
to shape our view of human progress.

1
What is Archaeology?

Today, our knowledge of the ancient world is almost entirely based on the evidence provided by archaeology. Before the middle of the nineteenth century, antiquarians based their knowledge of the ancients on written records, the writings of the early Greek, Roman and Jewish historians and geographers, and books such as the Bible. Literary evidence, however, is unreliable, for man often omits to tell the whole truth for a number of reasons. For example, he may see events through biased eyes, he may not be a good observer, or he may be basing his account of events on hearsay evidence, passed on by word of mouth, which may, in some cases, be hundreds of years old. Language again is a difficulty, as meanings tend to change with translation from one language to another. All these faults, however, did not daunt the early historians who wrote with absolute conviction. Chronologies were calculated and established which were looked upon as infallible facts. An example of this was the way in which the Old Testament was regarded as the only accurate account of ancient history, including its chronology.

In 1650, Archbishop Ussher published his *Annals of the Ancient and New Testaments* in which he asserted that the world began in 4004 B.C. Soon after, this date was not felt to be precise enough, and Dr John Lightfoot, master of St Catherine's College, Cambridge, made some obtuse and lengthy calculations, and announced that the world had indeed begun in 4004 B.C., on the 23rd October, at nine o'clock in the morning to be exact! He published this statement in a book entitled *A few and new observations on the Book of Genesis, the most of them certain, the rest probable, all harmless, strange and rarely heard of before*, a fitting title! However ridiculous the ideas of the early antiquaries and theologians, they were accepted at the time, and by the eighteenth century the date 4004 B.C. had been placed in the margin notes in the Bible, where it had an air of authority and therefore truth.

Not all antiquaries were satisfied with this state of affairs. Some realised that the situation was far from good and attempted to improve things. Men like William Stukeley and John Aubrey sought to supplement their knowledge with accurate field observation. John Aubrey, a Wiltshire squire, was the first observer to give a detailed description of Stonehenge and Avebury. In recognition, his name has been given to the pits which surround Stonehenge, a feature he first noted. Another pioneer of field archaeology was a Welshman by the name of Edward Llwyd, one-time Keeper of the Ashmolean Museum, Oxford. He travelled widely throughout Britain publishing the results of his work in a book called *Archaeologia Britannica*.

The nineteenth century saw a change in attitude. By then a number of antiquaries appreciated the sparsity of their knowledge and began asking awkward questions, which, at that time, could not be answered. Many suspected that the antiquity of man was extremely great and began to focus their attention on the stone implements of the 'pre-Roman period'. It was obvious to them that this period was very long, and contained a number of phases, but until some sort of order was established, the best they could do was to group it all together.

The breakthrough came not in Britain but in Denmark, where in 1816 Christian Jurgensen Thomsen, the Curator of the Danish National Museum, took the bold decision to arrange the collections in his museum according to kind. The antiquities were arranged in a Gallery of Stone, a Gallery of Bronze and a Gallery of Iron. Thomsen had taken note of the discussions and speculations current at the time that man's artefacts could be arranged by material, according to technological development. However, it was Thomsen's positive step that was the first major advance. His student, a man called Jan Jacob Rasmussen Worsaae, soon proved Thomsen's hypothesis by excavation, when he discovered arte-facts of the various phases in a stratified context, proving the order. Thus an order had been established, but no dates.

The way was now clear for other advanced thought. Soon Sir John Lubbock in his book *Prehistoric Times* pioneered the use of the terms 'prehistory' and 'prehistoric'. He also believed that the Stone Age could be divided into two. This he did and invented the terms 'Palaeolithic' and 'Neolithic' to describe the Old Stone Age and New Stone Age respectively.

It was becoming increasingly clear that in order to advance the know-ledge of ancient man, excavations had to be undertaken—excavations not simply to fill museum cases with curios, but to provide answers to many unsolved questions. Excavations of the former kind had been undertaken for some time in Britain, Europe and the Middle East, but what was needed was a more logical and scientific approach. It was at

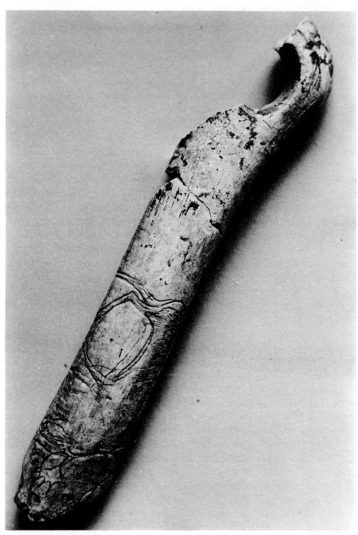

Palaeolithic engraving on a deer antler.

this time, in Britain, that men such as Pitt-Rivers appeared on the scene. Pitt-Rivers has often been called the father of modern archaeology and his excavations on Cranborne Chase in Dorset became a model on which future archaeologists based their work. He was a meticulous observer, and published his results in great detail.

The end of the nineteenth century really marked the beginning of modern archaeology—archaeology with a scientific approach. Once the change had been made to excavate for information and not for objects, the way lay wide open. Unfortunately, however, there are still some excavations, if they can be called such, that are carried out for the treasure hunting aspect, but they are few and far between.

The modern archaeologist looks for his answers in the soil, for he regards it as a giant history book, waiting to be read. However, any excavation, no matter how good, means destruction; it is like reading and perusing each page of a book, after which the page is destroyed. Therefore, every care has to be taken to ensure that not a scrap of evidence is lost, and that it has been correctly read. Contrary to popular belief, the pick and spade are not the trade marks of the archaeologist, but the trowel and brush. It is far better to scrape gradually through a few years of historic debris, than to bulldoze through hundreds.

An archaeologist has to use a variety of methods to collect his evidence. Typology and stratigraphy are his everyday tools and are important for establishing chronologies and evaluating cultural development. Modern archaeologists are able to use a number of scientific aids to help them, firstly to find and map sites, and secondly to date objects.

New discoveries are coming to the aid of the archaeologist every year, and it is therefore essential not to excavate all our sites, but to preserve some for excavation by future generations. In fact, this has been done in the case of Stonehenge, where an area has been especially set aside for this purpose. The danger today lies not in over-enthusiastic excavation of sites, but in their wholesale destruction by developments for roads and buildings, and new agricultural methods employed in the countryside. In spite of these threats, archaeology has come a long way from the days of John Aubrey, but it is still in its infancy. In the future, new archaeologists with new tools to aid them will no doubt add much to our ever-increasing knowledge of the ancient world.

2
Techniques—
Old and New

To many, archaeology still seems mere guess-work. This is an illusion, for today it has grown into what can best be described as a science, although some archaeologists may question this. There has always been a debate as to whether archaeology is a scientific art or an artistic science. Even as late as 1966, this debate was still raging. Nicolas Platon, the well-known Greek archaeologist, who has conducted important excavations in Crete, wrote: 'Archaeology is a science. It is not, as legend would have it, a fortuitous combination of luck and imagination. Like all sciences it is a product of human curiosity and reason. It uses precise methods aimed at achieving precise results. Its real purpose is not to fill the museums with startling, lavish and unusual exhibits, nor to provide spectacular excavation sites for the admiration of tourists. By painstaking research into the fascinating problems presented by the civilizations of the past it reaches farther and farther back into the mists of time and the very origins of the human race.'

Tom B. Jones, another archaeologist, in 1967 countered this by saying: 'The other misconception is that archaeology is a science. It is true that in archaeology measurements of various kinds are taken with great care, scientific methods and devices are used wherever possible, and a good archaeologist is as objective as his nature will permit, but the exactitude of the mathematical or physical sciences is rarely achieved, and frequently the archaeologist has to content himself with the crudest approximation.'

Today, the archaeologist utilises scientific techniques to such an extent that the only true definition can be that archaeology is a science. However, unlike most sciences, the results of archaeology can never be proved, but must always remain the most convincing interpretation of the facts available. Even written history cannot be proved; it is merely an observation, and observations can often be wrong.

How then, did archaeology begin? Archaeology began by the observation of physical remains obviously constructed by man, but in periods far removed from the observer. Initially, these antiquarian observers attempted to explain what they saw in terms of objects, things and events which were familiar to them. Hence, many of the writings of these early antiquaries are quite amusing, but nevertheless they must be recorded as the first attempt to understand man's past from the things he left behind him, rather than from any contemporary accounts which in many cases have not survived and in many others were not written.

These early antiquaries were influenced by classical writings and by popular folklore. However, it soon became obvious to all who involved themselves deeply in the study of human history through its physical remains that mere observation and speculation were inaccurate, or at least highly suspect. Antiquaries began to dig around some of the sites which had obvious physical remains and on others which they suspected, due to mounds of earth or other physical peculiarities, might contain evidence of early habitation.

At first, these early excavations, if excavations they can be called, were simply treasure-hunting exercises, which, due to the inadequacy of the methods they employed, could give little or no information about the people who made the objects they sought, or the period in which they were made. Identification of the objects was often haphazard and accurate dating non-existent. However, these early excavations represent a major step in the study of man's past because they brought to light objects made by men of other periods, indicating that man had a past, not written but very rich. This past could be revealed if techniques could be developed to provide information about the makers of the objects.

First, the study of these antiquaries was directed entirely at the objects, at the materials from which they were made, at the techniques by which their makers formed them, and at the decoration which was sometimes present on them. They were able, by comparison, to see a development and a relationship between materials of similar kinds, and between similar shapes and designs. Later, this technique of observation and comparison of objects developed into what we now call typology, that is the arrangement of related shapes in order of typological evolution. In other words, the early antiquaries found it possible to arrange similar objects in order of their development. In much the same way, if one was to assemble a whole line of Ford motor cars of different ages, it would be possible to arrange them in some chronological order by virtue of their technological and design development, thus arriving

Bronze Age burial urn of the 'Wessex Culture'.

at a plausible chronological sequence. However, without a date anchor, such a sequence may start at either end of the line, because it is possible for objects to degenerate as well as develop. Thus it became, and still is, very important for typological studies to have firm date anchors. But how were these anchors to be obtained? This was a most important question and until satisfactorily answered the study of archaeology could not advance.

Today, we have many techniques for providing date anchors, and the study of typology is still a very important tool for the archaeologist.

Providing a date anchor first came, and still often does, by observing that certain objects were found in context with a datable object, such as a coin on which a date was either inscribed or known; or an inscription; or in some cases through secondary relationships, for instance when an object such as a fragment or vessel can be dated because it had been found in other locations in association with typical material. The fragment can relate to the undated object with which it was found. But how could these early antiquaries be certain that the material found together had in fact been deposited together? They came up with a simple answer, which was only partially correct, but which established one of the most important tools that the archaeologist uses, that of stratigraphy.

When first applied, it certainly was not stratigraphy as we know it today, but was based upon the idea that the deeper the object, the older it was, and that any objects lying above it should be of a later date. In order to work to this method, the early archaeologists set up a datum point, a hypothetical level, from which they could measure the depths of all objects found in an excavation. This method allowed archaeologists to make great strides forward. However, it was far from accurate as there were many things that were not yet understood which could alter the date and relationship of the material. Like any natural geological stratigraphy, it does not follow that all the deposits would be perfectly horizontal, or that all the deposits would be undisturbed. They soon realised the inadequacies of the early datum line technique, and began observing the soil itself; it is this observation of the layers of the soil which is the basis of modern-day stratigraphical archaeology. By observing the various colourations of the layers of soil visible on the sides of their trenches, they could discern that there were in fact many layers, and that these layers were often intersected by disturbances of the layer above them. Thus many of the earlier results were shown to be spurious.

Soil deposits or layers are the accumulation of occupational debris and the natural build-up of hundreds of years. They represent in some cases the ruined walls of the buildings and ditches, post holes, pits, burials and other physical features which man could impose on his environment. In fact, the archaeologists found that they could read these layers like the layers of a cake. It was becoming obvious that the information they sought was written in the soil itself, and that to understand the significance of the finds, buildings, and physical remains they unearthed they had to be related to the soil which surrounded them.

17

Thus, it became possible to relate accurately objects found together in a stratigraphical context.

However, archaeological techniques could still only date objects by building up a complicated grid of relationships between material. But, the technique was extremely flexible, and through the fortunate discovery in Egypt of the King Lists found on papyri and frescoes, which could give documentary dates to stratified layers, the technique could be extended to date material as far back as the third millennium B.C. Until recently, this was the only method of dating which was available to archaeologists, but today science has come to their aid and they can now use a combination of methods to date sites, objects and periods. Among the most important of these techniques are radiocarbon dating, thermoluminescence and dendrochronology—the study of tree rings.

Radiocarbon dating works on the principle that every living organism absorbs radioactive elements of carbon, known as carbon 14. This process continues as long as the organism is alive, but when it dies it no longer takes in radiocarbon and, instead, the radiocarbon disintegrates at a fixed rate. The time it takes for half the radioactive element to disintegrate is known as its half-life, which in the case of radiocarbon is about 5,600 years. So, by measuring the amount of radiocarbon present in an organic specimen, it is possible to arrive at the date when the organism died. Thus it is possible to date any object made of an organic material, including bone, and by virtue of its relative position in the stratigraphy of the site, it is possible to date other objects found in context with organic material.

There is always an element of error in any radiocarbon date. It is a very sophisticated method requiring advanced technology and laboratory equipment. Because of the element of error, radiocarbon dates are always expressed with a $\pm$ figure. In recent years, it has been shown that there is considerable error in radiocarbon dates over a certain age, and scientists have arrived at a method of correcting this by recalibrating those dates from dates obtained by dendrochronological examination of the Bristle-cone pine, which grows at a high altitude in California. This recalibration of radiocarbon dates has necessitated the complete reappraisal of much of the ancient history of Europe, a process which is still continuing.

Another dating method now used as an important aid to the archaeologist is thermoluminescence dating. This process, however, can only be applied to pottery or to items of clay that have been fired. The technique is based on the principle that minute particles of uranium and thorium, contained in the clay of the pot, emit alpha particles, which are absorbed by the other minerals in the clay surrounding the radioactive impurities, causing ionisation and releasing electrons which are trapped in the body of the vessel. These electrons remain trapped at ordinary temperatures, but are released when heated, either during the original firing or subsequently, causing the emission of light. The reaction is continuous; thus the build-up of electrons increases with time, and in theory a vessel of greater age will have greater thermoluminescence. In other words, a sample of pottery or fired clay may be placed in a special machine at the laboratory and heated rapidly to a point at which it emits light. This light is measured and the degree of its intensity indicates the age of the sample.

The process of carrying out the test is very complicated, but the results obtained are generally accurate to within ± 10 to 15 per cent. Today, it is often employed to detect fakes, but it is an invaluable aid to the archaeologist confronted with unfamiliar examples of pottery. Once dated by this technique, it is possible to build up pottery sequences, which can themselves help to date specimens of other materials found in association with them in stratified layers.

The technique of dendrochronology is particularly interesting, for it is based on a simple idea with which everyone is familiar; that is, that generally speaking every year of a tree's growth is marked by a ring in its trunk. When a section is cut through a tree, it is possible to calculate its age by counting the number of rings. That is the simplest method of dendrochronology; however, it is quite unsuited to an archaeologist's purpose. Archaeological methods of dendrochronology are based on a deeper understanding of the growth of trees, for it has been discovered that, due to climatic variations, the amount of growth varies and this variation is detectable in the size of the rings. Over the years, the variation of climatic conditions causes a pattern of growth rings, a pattern which can be matched by wood from trees of different species of similar dates. Thus, it is possible by starting with a tree of say 100 or 200 years growth cut today to extend our patterns back for about 200 years. By finding wood from furniture, old buildings, and similar objects it is possible to extend this backwards by matching the patterns of overlaps. When the system is extended to link in with trees such as the Bristlecone pine, which lives for extremely long periods, it is possible to extend tree life dating to about 5,000 years.

Until comparatively recently, most archaeologists believed in the interpretation of human history from archaeological evidence on a 'diffusionist' basis. It was generally accepted that cultural and artistic ideas and technological innovations spread outwards from their point of origin, rather like the ripples in a pond after a pebble has been dropped in the water. Thus, it was thought that development of civilizations depended on interaction in order to spread ideas. One of the principle exponents of this diffusionist attitude was Gordon Childe. Recently, however, with the reappraisal of much of European history due to the recalibration of radiocarbon dates, Colin Renfrew has championed a new anti-diffusionist view. He asserts that the evidence now shows that technological innovations and inventions originated independently of each other at different geographical locations and at different times, without necessarily having either direct or indirect contact with other centres which had similar achievements. It may well be that both these attitudes are right, for while it is possible for inventions and innovations to occur independently of each other, this does not necessarily mean that some ideas were not spread by diffusion. For diffusion is still very much the basis for a great deal of archaeological interpretation.

Science today also aids archaeologists in field observations, for they no longer have to excavate a site in order to plan its layout. In some circumstances, quite an accurate plan of hidden features such as walls, ditches, pits, post holes etc. may be obtained by conducting a magnotometer or resitivity survey. A magnotometer measures the magnetic variation of the earth's surface, and any human disturbances are recorded in the reading. A resitivity survey measures the variations of the electrical resistance of the earth's surface and, again, any human disturbances are recorded in the reading.

The archaeologist first plots a grid over the site, then using one of these instruments takes readings above the intersections of the lines, recording them in a site book. These are then plotted on to a grid and any changes in the readings are noted and sometimes joined together in the same way as contours on a physical map. Sometimes, both a magnotometer and a resitivity survey are conducted on the same grid and the two plots used to supplement each other. The results can be quite accurate. They are not, however, an end in themselves, but are used to give the archaeologist an idea of what he may be able to expect, and he excavates the site in much the same way as a surgeon uses x-ray photographs before operating on a patient. Magnotometer and resitivity surveys, however, can only give an approximate plan of the site. It is still necessary to excavate to obtain an accurate plan.

Much of the archaeologist's aids are still personal, such as his eyes, for, on the whole, there is no substitute for accurate observation. Noting minute differences in the appearance of certain landscapes, the field archaeologist may often be able to assemble sufficient clues and dates to add to our knowledge of the past simply through observation. Obvious, but interesting, botanical variations that anyone should be able to spot are crop-marks. These are best seen from a high vantage point and are especially visible in times of drought.

Crop-marks are discolourations, usually lighter or darker than the surrounding area, which may outline structures such as walls or ditches, pits and even post holes. If there is a buried structure in a field then the mound of earth above the walls contains less moisture and is likely to dry out quicker than the surrounding soil. Thus, crops growing in a field containing such structures may appear lighter over the walls, due to either mild dehydration or, for the same reasons, less growth. Conversely, crops growing over ditches or post holes are generally able to draw upon a greater moisture content, and thus show darker in comparison to the surrounding crops, or grow taller. Archaeologists today employ aerial photographs to record these features and occasionally infra-red photography, which again may outline features hidden to the naked eye.

In the laboratory, technicians and scientists help the archaeologist by analysing the soil samples taken from excavations, giving detailed information of the geological build-up of the soil.

Also of great help is the biological and botanical information such as profiles of the ecology of the site, obtained by the examination of pollen and seeds which may, in suitable circumstances, be preserved in the soil. Detailed examination of bones have also come to the archaeologist's aid. So sophisticated are today's techniques that it is possible for an expert examining the remains of a human cremation to determine the age and sex of the individual and sometimes by careful examination of the bones (if present) to determine some of the diseases that the individual suffered, and sometimes even suggest the cause of death.

Today, then, science is the archaeologist's best friend, but logic and common sense must not be forsaken, for without these two very important factors science is of very little use. The archaeologist must use science and not allow science to use him. Techniques in archaeology are still, however, very much in their infancy, for true scientific archaeology is still less than a hundred years old and there is little doubt that, in the future, sites and problems that today's archaeologists find impossible to interpret will be solved by sophisticated techniques which today we can only anticipate.

3
Pioneers and Discoverers

For many years, the majority of archaeologists were amateurs—the appearance of the professional is only a recent phenomenon. In fact, the major archaeological discoveries have nearly all been made by amateurs, men and women not trained specifically as archaeologists, but who devoted either the whole or part of their time to the subject.

William Camden and John Aubrey were both gentlemen antiquaries, yet in their time they were the closest one could get to an archaeologist; Aubrey, in particular, was an excellent field observer. Both had a definite idea of what they were about. William Camden in 1586 described it in these words: 'In the study of Antiquity (which is always accompanied with dignity and hath certeyne resemblence with eternity) there is a sweet food of the mind well befitting such as are of honest and noble disposition'—a view which reflects his sincere belief in the search of ancient knowledge which was to be only the truth. The public, however, must have regarded these antiquaries with a certain amount of amusement, for John Aubrey, eighty-four years later, wrote: 'it is said of antiquaries that they wipe off the mouldinesse, they digge, and remove the rubbish'. Even Winckelmann, sometimes called the father of archaeology, was in no way a professional.

Johann Joachim Winckelmann, who was born in 1717, the son of a German cobbler, was principally a poet and man of letters with an overriding interest in the past. He became involved in the excavations at Pompeii, but he was more interested in the archaeological finds as works of art than as a testament of human history. The excavations at Pompeii were conducted by another amateur, an engineer by the name of Rocco Gioacchino de Alcubierre, who in 1748 began excavations on the site on the orders of King Charles III of Naples.

Also belonging to this period was Sir William Hamilton, the British Ambassador to Naples, famous for his collection of Greek vases in the British Museum. Part of the collection lay for years at the bottom of the sea, having been ship-wrecked, but it has now been recovered and the whole collection is in the British Museum. An antiquary with an insatiable desire for collecting, he added a great deal to our knowledge of ancient Greek art through his desire for knowledge and beautiful things. He is also well-known as the husband of Lady Hamilton, Nelson's lover.

In the nineteenth century, really great advances in archaeology were made by amateurs, but these advances were not always spectacular in the physical sense, for one of the greatest achievements of the century was the work carried out by John François Champollion in the decipherment of Egyptian hieroglyphic writing. Champollion's interest in Egypt was roused at an early age, and at sixteen he went to Paris where he studied a number of languages, including Hebrew, Syriac, Chaldean, Sanskrit, Persian, Arabic, Greek, and Coptic. With languages he was in his element especially when in 1808, while still in Paris, he was confronted with a copy of the Rosetta Stone, a basalt slab inscribed in hieroglyphic, demotic and Greek. The stone, which had originally been discovered by the French, had come into the hands of the English as part of the spoils of war, hence he could only examine a copy. Champollion's interest was fired by the inscriptions on the stone, as it was obvious to him that they could provide the clue to the unravelling of the hitherto undeciphered script of the ancient Egyptians. It is common knowledge today that he succeeded, and we can be forever thankful for his providing the key to a lost time.

A similar triumph of detective work was achieved by another amateur over one hundred years later, working on the clay tablets that had been unearthed from Sir Arthur Evans' excavations in Crete and other excavations carried out on the mainland of Greece at Mycenae. These tablets were inscribed in two similar scripts, known as Linear A and Linear B. In 1952, a young architect, Michael Ventriss, working in collaboration with John Chadwick, a don at Cambridge, succeeded in cracking the code to Linear B. It is interesting to reflect that Greek was a common link to both hieroglyphics and Linear B, though of course they are in no way connected. The Greek inscription on the Rosetta Stone helped to decipher Egyptian hieroglyphs, but in the case of Linear B no-one had even thought that the language of the tablets might be Greek. So, scholars throughout the world, including the transcribers themselves, were surprised to find that they were in fact written in an ancient form of Greek. The point of this is that Greek, although an ancient language, is known, and any decipherment of mysterious scripts can only be successful if they can be related to a known language. Therefore, even if one managed to transcribe correctly a text phonetically, if the language was not known, it would not tell us a thing. There is a remarkable difference between the information both these discoveries have given us, for the world of the ancient Egyptians has opened up dramatically, with the translations of the numerous papyri and stone inscriptions which record everything from trade, royal proclamations, religious and magical texts to letters etc. On the other hand, though, the Linear B texts are rather mundane, and have only given us an insight into the trade carried out in Minoan Crete, for no religious or literary documents of any kind have been found.

The nineteenth century gave the modern world much of the ancient world. Adventurers such as Austen Henry Layard discovered the ruins of ancient Nineveh and Babylon, and shipped vast stone statues, the handiwork of these cultures, back to his patrons at the British Museum. The world of the Bible began to be a real place, represented by real buildings and remains.

Perhaps the most bizarre and certainly the most colourful figure of early nineteenth century archaeology is Giovanni Battista Belzoni. Born in Padua in 1778, this Italian giant was the cowboy of archaeology. Perhaps he can best be described as a recoverer of antiquities no matter how large, for with swashbuckling thoroughness he moved everything from obelisks to giant statues, dragging them half-way across the desert to ship them to the British Museum in London. After studying for a short time in Rome, he left there in 1803 for England, where he spent nine years working in Music Halls and circuses as an Italian giant (he originally wanted to enter the Church). Sir Richard Burton described him as 'a magnificent specimen of a man, strong as Hercules, handsome as an Apollo'.

In 1815, after having invented a new kind of waterwheel, Belzoni left for Egypt, where he hoped he would be able to exploit his invention. He met with little success however, and was left stranded in Egypt without money. He soon recognised that, in a land rich in antiquities, this was his best source of finance, and with little delay attached himself to the British Consul-General in Egypt, Henry Salt, as a collector of Egyptian antiquities.

Belzoni did everything with force; if something stood in his way, even sealed doors of tombs, he broke them down with battering rams. In spite of these violent methods, however, his work was the most scientific undertaken in Egypt at that time, for he brought back numerous measurements, sketches and imprints. He left Egypt in 1819 for London, where he published his memoirs, entitled *Narrative of the Operations and Recent Discoveries Within the Pyramids, Temples, Tombs and Excavations in Egypt and Nubia.* He never returned to Egypt, but in 1823 made an expedition to find the site of Timbuktu; he died shortly after of dysentery, on the 3rd December, and was buried at Gwato in present-day Nigeria.

The latter part of the nineteenth century saw the arrival of archaeologists of a completely different calibre—men like Heinrich Schliemann, General Pitt-Rivers and Sir Flinders Petrie. While Pitt-Rivers conducted what can be described as the first scientific excavations on his estate at Cranborne Chase in Dorset, England, Schliemann, retiring from business at an early age after having made his fortune, directed his attention to finding the legendary cities of Troy and Mycenae. He believed that the great epics of Homer were based on fact, a point he was able to prove at both these sites since his careful detective work and excavations produced some of the most spectacular discoveries of the age. At Mycenae, he thought he had discovered the tomb of the legendary Agamemnon, for he was convinced that he was excavating in the period in which the legends of Homer were set. (This was later proved wrong and the layers he was excavating were in fact earlier than Homer.) On discovery of the tomb and the superb gold burial mask, he was so excited that he sent a telegram to the King of Greece saying that he had, that day, gazed upon the face of Agamemnon.

Of a more sedate character, though perhaps more colourful, was Sir Flinders Petrie, who carried out the most thorough excavations that had, up to that time, taken place in Egypt. He became a familiar figure in his excavation bus with his pith helmet and white beard and his published works are still regarded as an extremely important contribution to Egyptology.

Fired by the success of Schliemann's work in Mycenae and by an overwhelming curiosity for engraved seal-stones, which he had discovered in his museum, the Ashmolean, in Oxford, Sir Arthur Evans made comparable discoveries to Schliemann in Crete where he discovered at Knossos the legendary palace of King Minos, after which he named the Cretan civilization.

These men, however, were the last of a breed, for from the beginning of the twentieth century archaeology became more and more professional. Great discoveries, of course, were still made, but they were made principally by men and women trained in the discipline of archaeology. This brought about conflict, and a great deal of the problems encountered by Howard Carter on his excavation of the Tomb of Tutankhamun was due to his connection with a private sponsor, Lord Caernarvon.

In Mesopotamia, some of the finest archaeological work was carried out by Sir Leonard Woolley who found the legendary city of Ur with its spectacular Royal Tombs. Meanwhile on the other side of the world, in South America, Edward Herbert Thomson, one of the last great amateurs (he was for twenty years the U.S. Consul in the Yucatan), was fired by accounts of an early American traveller, John Lloyd Stevens, and set out to excavate some of the lost cities of the Mayas.

Perhaps the most colourful figure of twentieth century archaeology has been that of Sir Mortimer Wheeler, a true professional. In his long career, in which he laid down the basis for all future scientific archaeology, he discovered the Roman trading port of Arikamedu in South India, and became the first Director General of the Archaeological Survey of India, after having made important contributions in Britain such as the massive hill-fort of Maiden Castle in Dorset, England, and the site of Verulamium (near present-day St Albans) in Hertfordshire, England.

When reviewing the great personalities of archaeology we must not forget those who have made significant contributions, but not great and spectacular discoveries; men like Cyril Fox and O. G. S. Crawford, who have made major contributions to British archaeology, and V. G. Childe, who was a major prehistorian and theoretician. Nor should we forget the women such as Margaret Murray, a great Egyptologist, and Kathleen Kenyon, who discovered the ancient site of Jericho.

Archaeology has come a long way, but it is destined to go much, much further, and the men and women who make the major discoveries of the future will continue to be drawn both from the ranks of the professionals as well as occasionally from the vast body of amateurs the world over.

4
Africa—
The Beginnings

Africa can perhaps be described as the cradle of mankind—the birth-place of man. Compared with other continents and countries, she developed late and saw few civilizations comparable to others of the ancient world, and yet her history is long and her place in the development of mankind important. As a continent she is huge, for within her shores she encloses many races and climates, yet in spite of her size, or maybe because of her size and the inaccessibility of large areas, we know comparatively little of her ancient history.

In Africa, the most ancient antiquities are the physical remains of man's ancestors. In the 1930s a number of bone fragments were found which appeared to belong to an advanced species of ape. These primitive hominids are known as Australopithecines—'southern apes'. As time passed and more of the bone fragments were found, they appeared to be more like an extremely primitive form of man. The shape of their skull was different from that of an ape, their face was shorter and the brain dome higher and more rounded. Another non ape-like feature was the fact that they appeared to be upright creatures and capable of walking and standing erect, though to a lesser degree than modern man. Their jaws and teeth all exhibited non ape-like features, as did their feet. The discovery of the remains of a complete pelvis showed that the shape was almost completely human and not ape.

The remains of Australopithecines were found over a number of years at various sites in South Africa. Dr Raymond Dart, Professor at Witwatersrand University, Johannesburg, was the first to report the findings of a skull in a quarry at Taung in South Africa. Other remains were found in the Transvaal. Later, further remains were found at other sites in southern Africa, as well as on the banks of Lake Eyasi in Tanzania.

A sturdier form of Australopithecine was found by Dr Leakey in 1959 in the Olduvai Gorge. Because of the huge jaw he called it 'Nutcracker Man' or *Zinjanthropus*. Leakey also found the remains of *Homo habilis*, 'the Handyman', a creature far more akin to modern man. *Homo habilis*

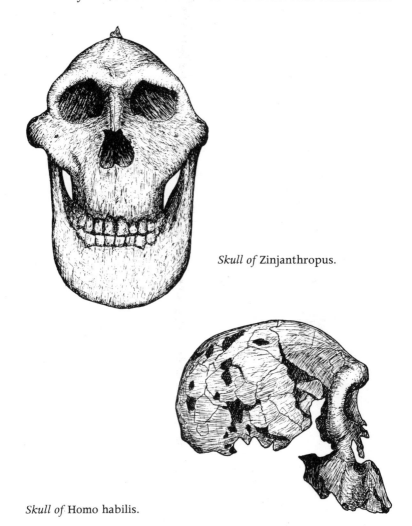

Skull of Zinjanthropus.

Skull of Homo habilis.

is almost the 'link man' between the Australopithecines and *Homo erectus*, another form of early man. Some scholars have likened *Homo habilis* to the Australopithecines, and others to *Homo erectus*. *Homo habilis* was rather short, only about four feet (1.2 m) in height. He was not muscular, and although his brain was much smaller than modern man's, it was about 100 c.c., larger than that of any known Australopithecine.

The development of man was not a continual process of one developing from another. Sometimes groups of primitive men existed alongside each other, competing for survival. This was the case with Australopithecine and early forms of men of habiline stock, collectively known as *Homo erectus*. Australopithecines lost the struggle for survival, while *erectus* prospered and spread into other areas of the world, eastwards to China and westwards to Europe.

Probably the oldest man-made objects are the stone tools from the Olduvai Gorge in Tanzania. These Oldowan tools, often called pebble tools because they were most commonly chipped from pebbles, were simply chipped in two directions on one side of a pebble; the result was a useful jagged cutting edge. The most common tool is the chopper. Although tools of this kind were first identified in the Olduvai Gorge, they have now been found all over Africa, including Ethiopia, Morocco

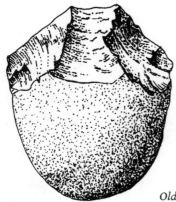

Oldowan chopper.

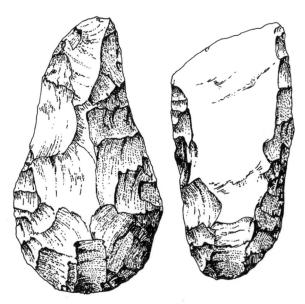

Acheulian Tools. Left: *hand-axe;* right: *cleaver.*

and Algeria. Similar tools have also been found in South East Asia. The Olduvai phase lasted for nearly one million years.

The hand-axe, an object familiar to archaeologists from Britain to India, had its home in Africa and is the product of *Homo erectus.* In 1960, Dr Leakey found a fossilised skull which was dated by the potassium-argon method to around 490,000 years ago. (The radioactive element in potassium-argon has a longer half-life than that of radiocarbon so, although open to larger errors, it can be used for dating much older bones.) The skull that Dr Leakey found was associated with hand axes of the Chellean type. The Acheulian type of hand-axe was also the product of *Homo erectus.* At the Olduvai Gorge, eleven stages of development of the Acheulian culture have been traced, and it is now possible to suggest that the culture lasted for nearly 500,000 years.

The early tools had an uneven cutting edge and were deeply flaked during their construction with stone hammers. Later, when tools were made with softer bone or wooden hammers, the implement became flatter with a straighter cutting edge, a far more efficient cutting tool.

31

Hand-axes were not hafted, but as their name suggests used in the hand, and made from a variety of stones depending on what was most readily available. In Europe they were nearly always of flint, but in Africa they were made from anything from dolerite to quartzite. Hand-axes were not the only tools of Acheulian man; he also made cleavers, with their straight cutting edge which was ideal for butchering, and also scraper and flake knives.

At Kalambo Falls, at the southern end of Lake Tanzania, Dr Desmond Clark has excavated four Acheulian camp sites. Wood from the late Acheulian level has given a radiocarbon date of 57,300 B.C. Shortly after this period, in about 50,000 B.C. the climate of Africa began to change, becoming arid. This forced men into different areas and environments, causing them to modify their activities and, together with the evolution of flaking techniques, caused new tools to be made. The Sangoan culture developed separately from the Late Acheulian; it was specially adapted to the new environment of forests and woodlands, while the late Acheulian adapted to the cool high plateau savannas. The typical tools of the Sangoan culture are rougher and cruder than the earlier Acheulian. The phase lasted some 10,000 years.

The Middle Stone Age lasted from about 40,000–15,000 years B.C.

Sangoan quartzite block scraper.

and was followed by the Late Stone Age, each period being characterised by its own tools. An interesting Late Stone Age site was found at Gwisho Hot Springs on the Lochinvar Ranch in Zambia. Here, in addition to the usual stone implements, remains of organic material were also found. The excavations on this site have helped to reconstruct an accurate picture of the time and we now know that the economy was based on hunting and food gathering. Using wooden arrowheads, the people hunted antelope, wart-hog, zebra and buffalo. They also collected nuts, seeds, roots and tubers, which were sometimes ground with grindstones.

The Late Stone Age in Africa gave way to the Iron Age, some 2,000 years ago, and the hunters and food gatherers were pushed from the agricultural lands by the Iron Age farmers. Today, their descendants, the bushmen of the Kalahari Desert, still live a similar life. With the Iron Age, a new chapter of African history opens. There is a complete economic, technological and cultural change, and technological innovations such as pottery, iron and agriculture appear almost simultaneously.

Several Iron Age villages have been excavated in Zambia, on the Batoka Plateau, and radiocarbon dates show that they were occupied from about 300 A.D. to 1000 A.D. A more interesting village, that of Ingombe Ilede, south of the Batoka Plateau, has been also excavated. This was a trading village yet several graves were found in the centre of the site with rich funerary goods, including gold, shell and glass necklaces, and also ceremonial hoes, copper crosses and gongs. Perhaps the most famous African ruins are those of Zimbabwe in Zimbabwe Rhodesia; these fantastic buildings were built on land first occupied by the Early Iron Age people in 300 A.D. The first stone structures were not built until 1000 A.D. Like other African 'civilizations' the 'golden age' of Zimbabwe was comparatively late in terms of human history, from 1440 A.D. to 1833 A.D.

From the artistic as well as technological point of view, perhaps one of the greatest African cultures was on the west coast of Africa at Benin. Here a sophisticated, though barbaric, culture developed and prospered from the sixteenth century until the late nineteenth century. The fantastic metal-working skill of the Benin artists produced some of the most beautiful of all African works of art.

The archaeology and cultures of Africa are fascinating for so many reasons, not least for their contrasts. On the one hand, we have the earliest appearance of man and yet on the other very little to show in

33

the way of development for such a long time. Perhaps the answer lies in the extremely hostile environment that man had to cope with, leaving him little time for other thoughts.

5
Mesopotamia—
The Fertile Crescent

The Fertile Crescent was the birthplace of Near Eastern civilization. It could also be called the birthplace of ancient history, for many of the stories in the Old Testament familiar to antiquaries had their origin in Mesopotamia.

In the flood plain of the Tigris and Euphrates rivers, near the Persian Gulf, developed one of the most sophisticated civilizations of the ancient world. From here its influence spread over a wide area and was felt as far afield as the west coast of India.

Most of the world's greatest civilizations began along the banks and alluvial plains of great rivers. In China it was the Yellow River, in India Indus, and in Egypt the Nile, the lifegiving properties of the flood plain making food production, and likewise life, that much easier. Time not spent on producing food could be utilized for religious, artistic or commercial enterprises. Thus, perhaps, the key to advancement was freedom from concern over food.

All great civilizations need a 'nursery' period, and the Sumerian was no exception. It grew from a simple, primitive culture, which we know today as Al 'Ubaid. The Sumerians were a non-Semitic and non-Indo-European people. The land on which the ancient sites of Ur, Eridu, Lagash, Larsa, Ubaid and Jamdat Nasr were built is all recent, formed in historical time. Originally the Persian Gulf penetrated far inland, but gradually the water receded, giving way to islands of dry land and, eventually, a flat fertile plain. It was a complicated action caused by river silting of the Euphrates and Tigris and a mud bar formed by two other rivers. The combined effect of this silting action resulted in land forming not at the north but at the extreme south. The story of Genesis was taken by the Hebrews from the original story of the Creation, handed down by the inhabitants of southern Mesopotamia. It recorded faithfully the action of the re-claiming of the land that took place. God said 'Let the waters under the heaven be gathered together unto one

Portrait of Gudea, governor of Lagash, Sumeria. From Lagash (modern Tello, southern Iraq), c. 2100 B.C.

36

place and let the dry land appear' and it was so. . . .

The areas of dry land were soon colonised by settlers from the east. The earliest phase is named after the site of Tell Al 'Ubaid, four miles (6.4 km) north of the ancient city of Ur. The phase is also present at Ur.

Sir Leonard Woolley, after excavating the famous Royal Cemetery at Ur, found the stratification separated from the upper levels by $8\frac{1}{2}$ (2.7 m) feet of sterile silt—the remains of a flood. Startled by this, he excavated another pit and confirmed his first findings. The Al 'Ubaid phase had been present in the site, but had been interrupted by a great flood. After the waters receded, the site was again settled. The people of this phase were in the late Stone Age; all their implements were of stone and their pottery was extremely fine and thin walled though hand-made without the aid of a wheel. The fired pots were decorated with geometric designs in brown or black on a white background. To this period belongs a distinctive type of female 'mother goddess' figure, some with child.

The Al 'Ubaid phase was followed by two other phases, the Uruk and the Jamdat Nasr, both named after sites where the phases were first identified. The Uruk people were from the north and were more advanced than the Al 'Ubaid, having the use of such materials as copper. Their pottery was no longer hand-made, but thrown on a wheel. They soon made themselves masters of the land, although the Al 'Ubaid people continued to live by their side. The Uruk phase was superseded by the Jamdat Nasr, another immigrant people, probably from the east. They were more sophisticated and had developed a system of writing using a pictographic script. Their pottery was painted and their phase can be described as the 'Early Dynastic Period'. The first of the graves in the Royal Cemetery were dug late in this period.

To the layman, the Royal Graves of Ur are probably the most spectacular feature of Mesopotamian archaeology. They were discovered by Sir Leonard Woolley, the director of a joint expedition to Mesopotamia by the British Museum and the University Museum of Pennsylvania. The site of Ur lies nearly midway between the Persian Gulf and Bagdad. Out of the desert wasteland rise the mounds which were once a noble city. The highest of these, the Ziggurat, is called by the Arabs 'Tel al Muqayya', the Mound of Pitch.

Excavations were first carried out on the Ziggurat as early as 1854 by J. E. Taylor, the British Consul at Basra, who was interested in collecting antiquities for the British Museum. It was he, in fact, who found an inscription which identified the mound as that of Ur of the Chaldees, the home of Abraham, though the inscription lay unread until much later. Some work was carried out on the site in 1918–1919, but excavations did not begin in earnest until Sir Leonard Woolley's excavation in 1922. The Ziggurat, the great land mark we see today, was built by Ur-Nammu of the third dynasty of Ur. The Ziggurat itself is one great history book, for within its many layers are preserved the remains of numerous periods of history, from Nebuchadnezzar to the Uruk and even earlier periods.

The Royal Cemetery was actually discovered by accident in 1922, but at that time Sir Leonard Woolley felt that neither he nor his workmen were sufficiently experienced to excavate it, so he delayed until 1927.

His judgement proved to be right, for the excavation was indeed difficult. Excavations showed that there were actually two cemeteries, one on top of the other, the top one dating from the period of Sargon of Akkad. The Royal Cemetery lay below. Many of the graves had been plundered, for, as in Egypt, the sumptuous burials proved a great attraction for tomb robbers. Not all the graves were royal, in fact only about sixteen were; the great majority of over two thousand were of commoners. Sir Leonard had to introduce many innovations into his excavation techniques to suit the conditions. Where wood had decayed and left a hollow, he poured in plaster of Paris to cast a replica, a process which sometimes produced spectacular results. On many occasions he was thus able to photograph how a wooden object would have looked originally, although in reality it was nothing but dust.

The richest and finest of the commoners' graves was that of Mes-kalam-dug, 'Hero of the Good Land'. In it was found a fine collection of gold, copper and electrum objects, the finest being a superb golden helmet in the form of a wig.

The Royal graves were extremely rich, as a result of which the majority had been plundered. Although each one differed from the other, human sacrifice was a feature common to all. Unlike the graves of commoners, nearly all were brick and stone lined tombs at the bottom of a shaft, with a sloping passage entrance. The sides were sometimes mud plastered and the floors and walls lined with matting.

Among the most complete was the burial of King A-bar-gi and that of his Queen Shub-ad immediately adjacent. Each interment had been accompanied by human sacrifice. Victims could number anything from six to eighty. The Royal occupant was usually accompanied by a few close attendants in his brick or stone lined tomb, the bulk of his court being buried just outside and sometimes underneath. The victims wore their finest court robes and seem to have gone into the tomb willingly. Most carried a small cup which may have contained poison or a knock-out drug. Both men and women were buried, court ladies, entertainers, soldiers, even chariot drivers together with their chariots and animals, either ox or ass. The animals were, of course, slaughtered before being buried.

The ritual that was associated with these burials was extremely complicated for it was not simply a matter of refilling the tomb with earth. Sir Leonard Woolley found it impossible to reconstruct this ritual of burial from one grave alone. Because of robbing, some were very badly damaged; however, an overall picture was obtained from the total excavated evidence. It seems that the king or queen was considered divine and death was merely a transformation from one world to the other; therefore, they would wish to be accompanied by their servants, who from all appearances went willingly.

After the attendants had been bricked up with the king or queen, the rest of the court would arrange themselves outside and the area would then be filled up with soil. On top of this there would be an offering to the gods, placed on a mat and protected by an inverted bowl. Above this a subterranean building would then be filled with a layer of clay, then a layer of offerings, together with a human victim, and so on in layers one on top of the other, until finally a chamber was constructed for the chief sacrifice and the building was sealed off. Each act would be accompanied by a religious ceremony and the whole burial would take some time.

We do not know the exact religious significance of the burials and ceremonies, only that later they changed and subsequent Royal burials were not as rich. The occupants of these tombs were kings before the first dynasty. They were kings of Ur, not Sumer; that came later.

Most of the very fine objects in the British Museum and the University Museum of Pennsylvania have come from the Royal Cemetery. Vast numbers of gold and silver cups, gold daggers, copper vessels, weapons including gold and silver spears, fine harps with the heads of bulls and other animals in copper, chariots, jewellery, head-dresses and alabaster vases—numerous objects have been recovered in spite of the plundering of the tombs.

There are many more periods represented at Ur, and many more sites in Mesopotamia. The civilization of this area continued to flower, but at the same time new centres to the north sprang up and other civilizations developed. Later, one of their kings, Nabonidus of Babylon, a keen antiquarian, took an interest in the ancient site of Ur and had it restored. He could perhaps be called the first Mesopotamian archaeologist.

6
Egypt

Perhaps the best known of all the material remains of man are those of ancient Egypt. As early as the fifth century B.C., men from other lands were marvelling at the magnificent colossi and buildings that the ancients had constructed. In about 450 B.C. the Greek geographer Herodotus included an account of his visit to the Nile Valley in Book II of his *History*, while later in about 250 B.C. the Egyptian priest/historian Manetho wrote his *History of Egypt* in Greek.

The Egyptians themselves greatly venerated their past and one could in fact call them the first Egyptologists. As early as the third millennium, they had begun to record their list of kings and major events. Manetho included in his history a list of kings from Menes in the First Dynasty to Alexander the Great. Tradition in ancient Egypt was all important; for example, a pharaoh wishing to commission new sculptures of deities or painted murals would probably seek out earlier works for his artisans to copy. The ancient Egyptian people also took delight in their past, and often paid visits to temples and tombs well over a thousand years old. Just like many modern visitors, they left scrawlings on walls to testify to the fact.

This rejoicing in the past, and their conservative approach to life, probably had an effect on their arts and crafts which resulted in the overall 'sameness' of Egyptian art. The 'Egyptian' appearance of antiquities is constant from the fourth millennium to the first centuries B.C. Herodotus himself describes scenes, customs and artefacts which must have originated centuries before. It is probably this easy identification of 'Egyptian things' which endears Egyptian archaeology to the layman today. The everyday articles, the ceremonial articles, perfectly preserved, can be related to his modern material culture, providing a bond between him and the past. In addition, there is another element of attraction, the mystery of religion and magic, and the ancient Egyptian's strong preoccupation with the preparation for death.

Mummification of the body was to the Egyptians an important part of religion, along with their belief in life after death. Early in Egyptian prehistory, the body was preserved quite naturally by burial in hot dry sand, which acted as an efficient dehydrating agent.

A good example of a body preserved in this way is 'Ginger', whose Pre-Dynastic burial is reconstructed beneath glass in the British Museum, although recently some doubts have been cast about his authenticity. It appears that during the nineteenth century the British Museum badly needed a Pre-Dynastic burial exhibit, and this need was dutifully filled by a rather notorious antiquities dealer, whose brother had disappeared in mysterious circumstances! The British Museum, however, is quite satisfied and is not willing to put 'Ginger' up to the test and sacrifice what may be a perfectly genuine exhibit.

Later, when burial became more sophisticated, entailing the use of a sort of chamber, this natural dehydration process could not take place. Experiments were carried out to overcome this, but it was not until the Fourth Dynasty (c. 2613–2494 B.C.) that the Egyptian embalmers realised that the most necessary step towards preservation of a body was the removal of the internal organs. Experiments, however, continued with a number of variations on a theme. The basic requirement, however, for successful mummification is dehydration, whether natural or artificial, and a stable environment.

It is this conscious approach to death by the Egyptians that has helped many of their artistic creations and artefacts to survive to the present day, sealed in the dry air-tight atmosphere of their tombs or pyramids or buried in the hot dry sand. Objects in wood, rush and other materials which in any other environment would have perished were preserved.

Probably most people's first introduction to the past is through the weird and wonderful remains of ancient Egypt. Most major museums have fine collections, and even the smallest manages to have, either on show or stored in its attics, antiquities that a tourist or early traveller acquired and brought home. People have been acquiring Egyptian relics for centuries, either by chance discovery, wholesale digging, purchase, or, as in the case of the famous Rosetta Stone, by war. Unlike other countries, Egypt has been fortunate to have such a wealth of history that sufficient remained for scientific excavation by modern archaeologists. It is the wholesale collection of the past centuries that has filled our museums, but it is the scientific excavations of the present day that has provided much of our knowledge.

It was Egypt's unique environment which enabled her civilization to flourish and develop. Egypt was like an oasis in the middle of the

Squatting figure of Sen-nefer, Royal Chancellor under the monarchs Hatshepsut and Tuthmosis III. From Thebes, 18th dynasty, c. 1500 B.C.

Egyptian sunk-relief in limestone. Head of a young man in the style of Akhenaten. From El Amarna, 18th dynasty, c. 1370 B.C.

desert of North Africa, as her crops were not at the mercy of the weather for a good or bad season. The Nile, which was the life source of this great empire, annually watered and fertilised the fields, its suspension of red silt giving at least one crop a season. Under the strong control of a centralised government, a portion of each year's harvest was stored for next year's seed, and also for times of need. The vast majority of the population were farmers whose work was continuous and largely concerned with irrigation, such as building dams, piercing dykes and watering the higher lying fields. Egypt at that time was a virtual paradise. Security and stability were provided in the form of the pharaoh, who as a living god-king linked politics and religion.

The country had a large population of domestic animals, and also had great natural resources. The land was rich with aromatic woods and resins and the deserts famous for their rich deposits of gold, natron, minerals and precious and semi-precious stones. Egypt was also a great centre of trade, supplying the commodities of tropical Africa to the lands of the Mediterranean, either in their raw state or manufactured into consumer goods by the almost unequalled skill of the Egyptian craftsmen.

The Egyptians were great artisans and artists, though somewhat conservative for they often worked to strict religious and artistic rules. On the whole, pottery was neglected as a medium for artistic expression. Much of it was mundane, with the exception of the Pre-Dynastic, highly burnished black top ware, which is simple and pleasing to the modern eye, the Pre-Dynastic painted Gerzean ware, and the fine, painted pots of the eighteenth Dynasty from Tel Amarna, made during the great cultural revolution of the pharaoh Akhenaten.

To the Amarna period of Akhenaten belongs some of the most interesting sculpture. It is notably different in style from both earlier and later works. Sculpture, both in the round and in relief, was one of the greatest artistic outlets of the Egyptians for millennia. Subjects were mainly religious or royal and ranged from small relief carvings to great colossi.

Apart from the great architectural remains of temples and palaces, much of the material remains of the Egyptians have come from tombs. The elaborate precautions taken to preserve the body after death also preserved many thousands of everyday objects, and exceptional objects of great beauty and intrinsic value, which were included with the deceased. Because of this, tombs when excavated by archaeologists were often found to be empty or ransacked. They had been the target for tomb-robbers for thousands of years, so it is not surprising that the discovery of the intact tomb of Tutankhamun with all the fantastic trappings of a royal funeral caused such a stir in 1922 and has continued to be considered almost the symbol of Egyptology ever since. The mummy of Tutankhamun was intact, although not in as good a condition as the excavators had hoped. There are few royal mummies that

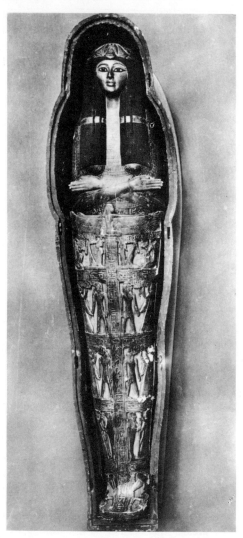

Mummy cover and coffin of Henutmehit, a priestess of the god Amun. From Thebes, 18th to 19th dynasties, c. 1300 B.C.

survive today, which have not at some time or other been rifled by robbers, who in their frantic search for jewels and gold have torn the wrappings and left the corpse damaged and exposed to the atmosphere.

Also from tombs comes one of the most familiar of Egyptian antiquities, the Ushabti figure. These little figures, made in various materials, wood or pottery, but most commonly in faience, were included in the tomb to act as the deputy of the deceased in the nether world and perform the menial tasks the deceased would be called upon to carry out. Most are inscribed in hieroglyphics with the name of the deceased and a magic inscription from the Book of the Dead.

With the Greek and Roman occupation of Egypt, a civilization and culture that had lasted for centuries declined and fell into decadence. Only buildings and sculptures remained, standing majestically aloof, testifying to the glories of the past. Today, the wonderful objects in our museums will forever evoke the eternal mystery of Egypt, a mystery that archaeologists for generations will seek to solve.

7
Ancient Near East

The ancient Near East was the melting pot of civilization. After the period of the Royal Tombs of Ur, the Sumerian culture continued to develop and to spread and its influences were felt far and wide. From this original stimulus and model, other civilizations in other parts of the Near East grew.

The development of civilizations is rather like the course of the common cold. It grows to a peak and then declines, but while it is growing it can 'infect' others. Thus the seed of civilization is passed from one culture to another, each one in its turn blooming and then wilting. The timing of this process of growth and decline may differ between civilizations; some may develop and decline quickly, others take a long period of development, and it sometimes happened that the stimulus of one civilization caused the development of another which grew up and flourished alongside it.

The Royal Tombs of Ur were the elaborate burials of the Kings of Ur. Later, as some of the cities gained ascendancy over the others, the King of the city became the ruler of Sumer. The Kings of Ur became Kings of Sumer around 2650 B.C. Later, Ur was defeated in battle and the city of Lagash became supreme. She in turn was replaced by Akkad, after being overthrown by Prince Sargon who reigned from about 2371–2316 B.C. during which he built a mighty empire. He was extremely powerful and, not content with ruling the whole of Mesopotamia, he sent an expedition across the Persian Gulf. After his death, the empire began to break up, as none of his successors were strong enough to protect it and keep it together. About 2230 B.C. it again reverted to city states which were in turn conquered by the King of Uruk in about 2120 B.C. His rule only lasted seven years, however, as he was defeated by the ruler of Ur who had regained control of Mesopotamia, although only for a short time until 2006 B.C.

The literature of ancient Mesopotamia was rich, many of the stories being adapted by the Hebrews and written down in the Old Testament. On the many cuneiform clay tablets that lie in the major museums of the

Copper figure of a bison. Sumerian work from Van (eastern Turkey), c. 2500 B.C.

world, in particular the British Museum, the story of the Flood, the Creation and many other events are recorded. The story of the birth and death of Sargon of Akkad himself closely resembles that of Moses. The inscription on a fragment of a clay tablet in the British Museum states that Sargon was brought forth in secret and was put by his mother into an ark of reeds smeared with bitumen, which she set floating on the river Euphrates. Akki, a water carrier, found the child and reared him, until the goddess Ishtar, having seen him, loved him and made him king over the whole land. Much of the ancient history of the Near East is told in some form or other in the Old Testament.

After the fall of Ur in 2006 B.C. her empire was split up and divided between six kingdoms, with their capitals of Larsa, Isin, Babylon, Eshnunna, Assur and Mari. There was now, however, a major political change. Whereas before life revolved around the gods and priest-kings, all wealth and land belonging to the gods, the land was given to the people and in contrast there was a free society.

For over two hundred years after the fall of Ur, the six kingdoms flourished. With inter-state rivalry, one kingdom would gain power over another, and land would change possession, and so on. The possessions of the six kingdoms stretched from the Mediterranean to the Persian Gulf. A change was to come when Hammurabi became King of Babylon in 1792 B.C. One by one, he captured the other kingdoms, until finally, with the fall of Assyria, in 1756, he ruled them all.

Although a small city, Babylon, by virtue of its position on the east bank of the Euphrates, was in a very strong strategic position where she could control traffic on both the Tigris and Euphrates. By wise government Hammurabi expanded Babylonian influence. He organised a system of government in which the governors of his empire were directly responsible to him, while each city had a 'Council of Elders' to decide local issues. Hammurabi was a great law giver; he gave judgement based on earlier precedents and had his own judgements recorded on clay tablets. Over two hundred and eighty two of his laws were carved on a stone monument and set up in the temple of the sun god, in Sippar. After Hammurabi's death, his kingdom broke up and what followed over the next centuries was rather chaotic and complicated.

In Asia Minor, as in Mesopotamia, civilization had flourished. An Indo-European people called the Hittites had established themselves and founded the Old Hittite Kingdom in about 1750 B.C. The Hittites were a war-like people with expansionist policies and they soon moved southwards to other lands. Meanwhile, in the south east, another warrior nation, the Kassites, were moving north west. In 1595 B.C. the Hittites thrust southwards, following the line of the Euphrates, and sacked Babylon. They did not stay, however, but withdrew, taking their plunder with them. The vacuum they left was filled by the Kassites, who ruled Mesopotamia until 1162 B.C. Another change took place in the area when the Kingdom of the Hurrians was infiltrated and taken over by the Mitanni, another Indo-European people.

In the fourteenth century B.C. major changes took place, for Egypt had conquered Syria. Then in 1372 B.C. the Hittites under Suppilulmus raided Egyptian Syria and at the same time plundered the Mitannian capital of Washukani. Later, there was internal trouble between the

Part of a stone tablet recording the re-foundation of the Temple of the Sun God at Sippar, Babylonia, by Nabu-apel-iddina. 9th century B.C.

Mitannians themselves, and the Assyrians and Hurrians joined in for good measure. The result was that the Assyrians regained their independence, controlling the southern part of the Mitannian Kingdom, while the Hittites controlled the northern part.

The Assyrians were a war-like people who regularly raided and attacked the surrounding lands. The first great Kings of Assyria were Ashurnasirpal II and Shalmaneser III, who carried out military campaigns extending over a wide area from the Persian Gulf to Palestine. With the death of Shalmaneser, Assyrian power declined while that of the neighbouring Kingdom of Urartu, which was based on slavery, grew.

When the Assyrian King Tigathpileser III (745–727 B.C.) came to the throne he set about re-establishing Assyrian supremacy. He re-organised his army, placed it on a professional footing, and began conquering new lands. Like the old Babylonian Empire Tigathpileser organised his empire with governors of each province responsible directly to him. It was their task to ensure that taxes and tribute were paid and to maintain law and order. Tigathpileser defeated Sardur II of Urartu and further extended the Assyrian Empire.

Later King Sargon II also had ambitions of empire, a fact illustrated by his assumption of the name of the founder of the Akkadian empire. Sargon conquered both Syria and Palestine, and even Cyprus swore allegiance to Assyria. Luck was not on Sargon's side, however, and he was killed in 705 B.C.

Sargon's successors were preoccupied with maintaining the empire that he had conquered and put down several revolts. Sennacherib (704–681 B.C.) sacked the ancient city of Babylon; this horrified his son so much that he murdered him while he was at prayer. Sennacherib's youngest son, Esarhaddin, then retaliated by driving out his brother. He then rebuilt Babylon, strengthening his position in the south. He held the advance of the Scythians in the north and in 671 B.C. conquered Egypt.

Esarhaddin was succeeded by his son Ashurbanipal. At this time there was almost constant warfare, rebellion and counter-rebellion and much of Ashurbanipal's time was taken up maintaining his empire. He died in 631 B.C.

Civil war wrecked Assyria and in 626 B.C. Nabopollassar, the governor of Babylon, revolted and set up the New Babylonian Dynasty. In 612 B.C. Nineveh, Ashurbanipal's capital, was sacked. So ended the Assyrian empire and with it the era of the early civilization of the Near

East. Later, other civilizations such as those of the Medes and the Persians took over, while earlier in the Levant other civilizations comparable to those of Mesopotamia had developed.

Each of the Assyrian Kings built his own capital city. Ashurnasirpal established himself at Calah, Sargon built himself 'The City of Sargon', Dar-Sharrukin, while other kings had capitals at Assur and Nineveh.

The remains of the great Assyrian cities were discovered in the nine-

Stone bas-relief showing Ashurnasirpal II being anointed by, perhaps, a priest, dressed in the head and wings of an eagle. From Nimroud (Calah), 883–859 B.C.

teenth century by an Englishman, Austen Henry Layard. He first excavated the city of Nimroud, Ashurnasirpal's Calah, then Nineveh. He
published the results in 1849 in his *Nineveh and its Remains*. Later he
excavated at Assur and Dar-Sharrukin. The account of his excavation
is fascinating to read for although he uncovered so much of archaeological interest, his motives were to recover specimens of ancient art.
Nevertheless, it was men like him who paved the way for the archaeologists of today.

*Sculpture in bas-relief of a lioness wounded in a hunting scene of Ashur-
banipal, King of Assyria. From Nineveh 668–630 B.C.*

8
Minoan Crete

The island of Crete has sometimes been called the jewel of the Aegean. It is a treasure house of antiquity, for within its shores lie the remains of thousands of years of history, dating from the Neolithic period to the present day. The history of Crete has certainly not been passive; on the contrary, it has been vibrant. It has been influenced by other civilizations as well as influencing others.

Until the turn of the century, however, much of its ancient history was unknown. The later periods from the time when it was a Roman province were well known, and well documented, but anything earlier was misty, unclear and uncertain. To scholars, stories of its ancient heroes were simply legends. Even the Romans had no idea of the great civilization that had preceded them.

After the discovery of Homer's legendary city of Troy and the ancient tombs of Mycenae by Heinrich Schliemann, some scholars began to entertain the idea that the Cretan legends may have had some basis of fact. Among them was Heinrich Schliemann himself who wanted to dig on the island, but in fact only conducted a small trial excavation.

The story of the discovery of the great Bronze Age civilization is interesting in itself. Arthur Evans, Keeper at the Ashmolean Museum, Oxford, had grown extremely interested in a collection of unusual seal-stones at the Museum which were engraved with pictographic signs. He wanted to find out where they had come from and learn more about them and the pictographs that covered them. His search eventually led him to Athens, where he purchased further seals from antiquity dealers. After much persuasion, no doubt monetary, he was able to learn that the seals had come from the island of Crete. There, the seals which were called 'milk stones' were collected in large numbers by the local peasants.

In 1893 Arthur Evans visited Crete where he learnt that great numbers of these seals were found at a site called Knossos, just outside Candia (present day Heraclion). A local amateur archaeologist named Minos Kalokairinos had already found and excavated a storeroom of a building at the site. Being a man of means, he purchased part of the site and in 1897 the Turkish authorities, who then ruled the island, gave him permission to excavate.

The Cretan rebellion, however, prevented the work from starting until the island gained her independence. The new Cretan authorities were sympathetic to Evans' cause and after negotiations he was able to purchase a further area of the site and confirm his ownership of the site. After gathering together his team, he started excavating. His original aim was to find further examples of the script that had brought him to the island. His wish was granted, for within a few weeks of the start of the excavation he had unearthed a large collection of clay tablets, but these were inscribed with an altogether different script, not the pictographs he had encountered on his seal-stones. His quest was soon diverted, however, for in his search for this mysterious script he found the remains of a new civilization, a civilization which antedated all others. He called it Minoan, after the legendary King Minos of Crete.

After further excavation, Evans was able to recognise three different scripts, the hieroglyphs and two cursive scripts which he called Linear A and Linear B. Although Evans was still interested in the task of deciphering the scripts, he was side-tracked into excavating and restoring the site of Knossos. These mysterious writings puzzled scholars and laymen alike until in 1952 one of the scripts, Linear B, was deciphered by Michael Ventris, a young architect working with John Chadwick. The result of his decipherment caused a great stir in the academic world, as he showed that the language of Linear B tablets was an early form of Greek. Evans' pictographs and the Linear A script, however, still remain undeciphered and a challenge to future archaeologists.

The new Minoan civilization that Evans discovered proved to be one of the most advanced that had ever been discovered. With its discovery, there was much speculation that Plato's account of the legendary island Atlantis might even refer to Crete. A number of books have been written in an attempt to associate the two. The most recent and scholarly is by Lucas.

The remains which Arthur Evans uncovered showed that the Minoan civilization extended over a long period, with a number of phases. Excavations by other archaeologists in different parts of the island confirm this. Evans was able to identify specific groups of objects and pottery with certain periods in stratified sequences. He divided the Minoan Culture into Early Minoan, Middle Minoan and Late Minoan, with subdivisions of each.

The earliest inhabitants of Crete were of Neolithic stock. They migrated to the island, probably from Anatolia in the fourth millennium B.C., using primitive boats to hug the mainland, then continued from island to island. On Crete there is almost a complete cultural continuity and it is possible to see the Minoan Bronze Age cultures develop from the Neolithic.

There are a number of theories on the dating of the various Minoan phases. The dates used here are those of Hutchinson. The Early Minoan Period lasted for a short time from 2500–2400 B.C. Remains of this period as a whole are scarce and at some sites such as Phaistos, pottery of this period is almost completely absent, while at Knossos it is rare. No copper tools of this date have been found. The Early Minoan II Period extended from 2300–2100 B.C. while the Early Minoan III Period, probably a very short transition period, lasted from about 2100–2000 B.C. During the latter period, copper implements and objects were made, but they are not common. Fine gold and silver jewellery has been found in graves dating to the early Minoan II to early Minoan III Period. This period also saw the beginning of Minoan ivory sculpture, but perhaps the finest artistic achievement of the Early Minoan II Period was the carving of stone vessels.

Evans was able to show that the Early Minoan Period was characterised by village life and was comparatively unsophisticated. This contrasts strongly with the conditions in the Middle Minoan Period, when life became much more sophisticated with large urban communities, cities and palaces. In this period it is clear from excavated evidence that there was a lively sea trade with Anatolia, Egypt, Syria and the Greek mainland.

The Middle Minoan Period saw the foundation of the great palace of Minos at Knossos. It was this palace that so enthralled Sir Arthur Evans that he spent the remainder of his life excavating and restoring it. The plan is a maze of intercommunicating rooms, surrounding a central court. Architecturally, the building is one of the most impressive and advanced in the ancient world. Perhaps the most interesting feature is the sewage and drainage system, a system that was extremely advanced and thousands of years ahead of its time. One room, known as the 'Queen's Lavatory' was even equipped with a wooden seat, and a special system of flushing and drainage. Although the Palace was extremely large, the rooms were inclined to be rather small. Many of the rooms were exquisitely decorated with painted frescoes.

Apart from the Palace of Knossos, there were also palaces at Phaistos, Mallis, and Gournia. The Middle Minoan Age was the golden age of

Crete, lasting from about 1950 B.C. to about 1550 B.C. About 1570 B.C. there was a catastrophe when a great earthquake with its epicentre situated on the nearby island of Thera, shook Knossos and badly damaged the palace. This calamity caused extensive damage to property and loss of life. It was a warning of worse to come.

The Phaistos disc. Crete, 17th century B.C.

During the first years of the Late Minoan Period, a great deal of reconstruction work was carried out. But although it started well, the Late Minoan Period marked the beginning of the decline of Cretan power. During this period also, the associated city of Mycenae on the mainland began to influence Crete, rather than be influenced by the Island. The period is marked by the appearance of extremely fine pottery.

The end of the Minoan Empire was dramatic and terrible. At about 1500 B.C. the volcano Thera began to grow restless, probably causing a number of minor quakes. Then about 1400 B.C. it reacted violently and blew up, causing part of it to submerge, leaving three islands. Parts of Thera itself are buried under thirty metres of volcanic ash and pumice. Thera is about sixty miles (100 km) north of Crete and the result of this eruption would have caused havoc and great destruction. The originator of this theory, the Greek archaeologist Spiro Marinatos, has compared the Thera quake with that of Krakatoa in South East Asia in 1883 A.D. The Krakatoa quake, although smaller than Thera, caused a series of great tidal waves which hit neighbouring islands, killing over 36,000 people. Calculations have shown that the Thera quake would have been even more disastrous, as indeed it was, for it destroyed practically all the centres of civilization on Crete. The Minoan culture survived in a somewhat decadent form, but the flower of Minoan civilization had been obliterated, and the palaces were never rebuilt.

From the excavated remains, we can now see that the old legends of Crete were not so far fetched as had been thought, and that they were founded, partly, on fact. The story of the Minotaur, literally the Bull of Minos, seems to have sprung up from elements of the Cretan religion. The bull was sacred, and we know from frescoes and models that religious bull games were held in the centre courtyards of the palaces where young men and women would vault over the back of a bull. It was a dangerous game and would probably have claimed the lives of numerous young men and women. As the courtyard where the games were held was in the centre of the palace, with numerous interconnecting rooms surrounding it, it became the legendary labyrinth with the bull headed monster in the centre waiting to consume the flower of youth. So Schliemann's theory that not all legend of the ancient world was fiction again seems to have been proved.

Excavations continue to add to our knowledge of the island's past, but Crete holds many secrets and may never fully reveal all.

9
Malta

The antiquities of Malta are many and varied; and the island has one of the highest concentrations of Megalithic art in Europe.

Man first settled in Malta during the fifth millennium B.C. after crossing the sea from Sicily. His first settlements left little remains and it is only recently that an early village site has been excavated at Li Skorba near the modern village of Mgarr.

The earliest pottery is dull grey clay with impressed designs known as Ghar Dalam ware, named after the site where it was first found. Later during the fourth millennium B.C., the pottery changed to a burnished grey ware, Grey Skorba (3600 B.C.), and then to a burnished red ware, Red Skorba (3400 B.C.). Remains other than fragmentary pots are rare and the only notable object of artistic merit of this period is a terracotta figurine. The pottery, however, is extremely graceful. Peculiar vessels known as 'ladles' often remind one of the 'sauce boat' vessels of Helladic Greece.

Before the period of the large megalithic temples, with their beautiful reliefs and weird figures of goddesses, was a short intermediate phase when pottery was both painted and decorated with incised lines and jabs. This period derives its name from a group of tombs at Zebbug, where it was first discovered. To it belongs an interesting, but puzzling, limestone head of a statue menhir. It is the oldest carving yet discovered in this group of islands, and dates to the early fourth millennium B.C. The face is long and oval, with the features suggested by two vertical incised lines and holes. This is unique in Malta, and therefore no local comparisons can be made except perhaps for the human figures on some pottery, and we have to look to Sicily, France, Iberia and perhaps the Eastern Mediterranean for any comparable examples, although none of them display a great degree of similarity. It must, therefore, be considered an indigenous creation.

Perhaps one of the most puzzling aspects of Maltese archaeology is the megalithic culture. Early in the third millennium B.C., the inhabitants of Malta had begun to erect great edifices of stone. At first they

1 Cleaning the stone foundations at the Winchester, Hampshire, excavations. This
was a massive urban archaeological project.

2 An emergency excavation. Archaeologists racing against a bulldozer at an Iron Age site, Bournemouth, Dorset.

3 Excavating the banks of the hill fort of South Cadbury, the supposed site of King Arthur's Camelot.

4 Section through a large ditch on an Iron Age site showing the successive cuttings and filling, identifiable by the different colours of the soil.

5 Mapping a site with the aid of a metric grid.

6 The Winchester Cathedral 'dig' employed numerous helpers from different countries. Labels indicate specific finds or layers.

7 An Acheulian flint hand-axe about 200,000 years old. The sharp edges have been dulled by glacial action.

8 Excavation of Roman buildings at Dorchester. The piles of tiles in the foreground are the remains of a hypocaust central heating system.

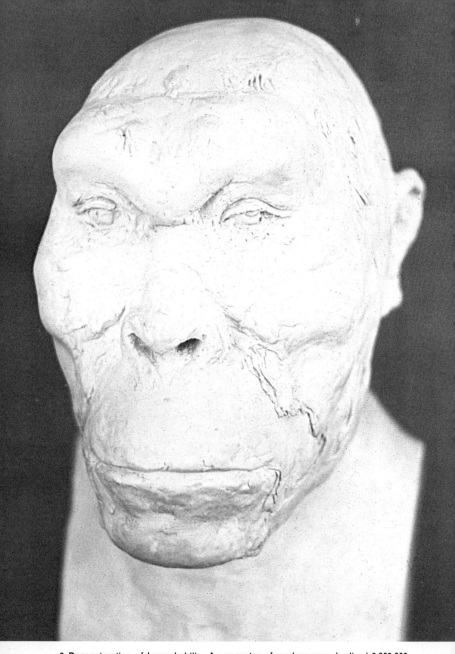

9 Reconstruction of homo habilis. An ancestor of modern man, he lived 2,000,000 years ago.

10 Palaeolithic cave painting of a bison at Lascaux, France.

11 Pictorial mosaic standard of a royal banquet in lapis lazuli and shell. From Ur, c. 2,500 B.C.

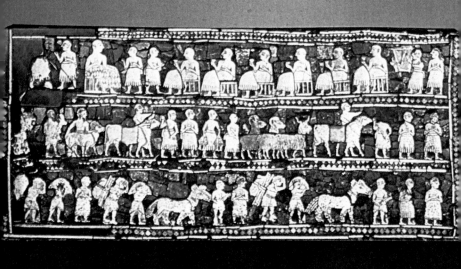

12 Bronze foundation figure from Langash, Mesopotamia, *c.* 2,125 B.C.

13 A group of Egyptian pre-dynastic black-topped pottery vessels. 4,000 B.C.

14 Egyptian painting from the tomb of Nebamun, showing guests feasting at a banquet. 1,400 B.C.

15 Gold death mask of Tutankhamun.

16 A pre-dynastic 'mummy' in the British Museum, London, nicknamed 'Ginger'.

17 Egyptian 'mummy' mask. Ptolemaic period, *c.* 600 B.C.

18 Egyptian painting of the Pharaoh Amenophis I from the tomb of Kynebu, a priestly
official of the late twentieth dynasty. 1,150 B.C.

19 The Rosetta Stone – inscribed in hieroglyphic at the top, hieratic in the middle and Greek at the bottom.

20 A shallow limestone relief of Nefertiti wife of Akhenaten, from Tel Amarna, *c.* 1,370 B.C.

21 Relief sculpture at Persepolis, showing Darius and Xerxes receiving homage.

22 Gilgamesh Flood tablet from Ashurbanipal's library at Nineveh. 7th century B.C.

23 A stone stela with cuneiform inscriptions, showing Ashurbanipal. Babylon, 7th century B.C.

24 Late Minoan pottery vessel decorated with marine abstract designs inspired by the sea. 1,500 B.C.

25 Minoan pottery pitcher decorated with marine abstract designs, the body also inspired by the form of a sea urchin. 1,500 B.C.

26 A steatite (soapstone) rhyton (drinking cup) in the form of a bull's head with golden horns. From the palace of Zakro, Crete. 1,500 B.C.

27 A view of the palace at Knossos, Crete. The trabeated doorway is a modern concrete reconstruction.

28 Entrance to inner sanctum of megalithic temple of Mnaidra, Malta. The 'pitting' was intended only as an anchor to hold painted plaster. 2,400 B.C.

29 Headless limestone figurine of mother goddess from Malta. These statues have been found in various sizes at some of the megalithic temple sites.

30 Roman mosaic floor from the Roman villa at Rabat, Malta.

31 Part of the interior of the Hypogeum or underground temple ossuary on the island of Malta. To the right are the remains of a painted ceiling.

32 A helmet-shaped vase excavated from the megalithic temple of Tarxien, Malta.

33 Relief carvings at the megalithic temple of Tarxien, Malta, c. 2,200 B.C. The carving of rams is unique, the norm being curvilinear motifs.

34 A Hellenistic terracotta figurine of Apollo, *c.* 3rd century B.C.

35 The Temple of Apollo at Delos. Built in the Doric style, the temple was not completed until the 3rd century B.C.

36 A marble sculpture of a leopard at the Temple of Apollo, Delos.

37 An Attic red-figured amphora showing a libation ritual. 450 B.C.

38 The Great Theatre at Ephesus.

39 A gold Thracian pectoral ornament from Duvanli, *c.* 400 B.C.

40 Thracian metalwork, *c.* 3rd century B.C.

41 A Greek Attic miniature oenochro in the form of a woman's head, 500 B.C.

42 The cells under the main floor of the Colosseum in Rome. Christians were not in fact thrown to the lions here, but in the Circus Caligulas.

43 A view of one of the streets in Pompeii. The chariot ruts are visible as grass-covered lines down the centre of the street.

44 A view of the Forum in Rome.

45 A black pottery vessel showing gladiatorial combat, excavated at Colchester, England.

46 The hypocaust central heating system at the Roman baths in Bath, England. The floor was supported by the piles of terracotta tiles.

47 The central medallion of the Hinton St. Mary mosaic, showing a figure of Christ flanked by two pomegranates. It is now in the British Museum, London.

48 Group of Samian and red-coated pottery together with other Roman earthenware vessels – part of the funerary furniture found in a Roman cremation.

49 The interior of the West Kennet Long Barrow, Wiltshire. The structure, which is Neolithic, shows the central passage and part of the corbelled roof.

50 A Bronze Age collared burial urn excavated from Stanpit Marsh, Hampshire.
Dating to c. 900 B.C., the urn contained the remains of a six-year-old child.

51 A bronze hanging bowl from the Sutton Hoo ship burial, *c.* 6th century.

52 An aerial photograph of Avebury, Wiltshire. This Neolithic tribal centre today contains part of the modern village of Avebury.

53 A Roman burial discovered during the excavations of the Fishbourne Roman palace at Chichester, Sussex.

54 A gold and enamel clasp found at the Sutton Hoo ship burial.

55 A red sandstone head of Siva from Mathura, India, *c.* 4th century A.D.

56 An Indian terracotta plaque of a woman with ornate head-dress. Sunga period,
c. 200 B.C.

57 View of the ruins of the Buddhist monastery at the Deer Park at Sarnath, near Benares, India.

58 Chinese terracotta figure of a lion of the Hui-hshien group. Han dynasty.

59 A reconstruction of the skull of Lantien man found at Lantien, Shansi, China, in 1963, *c.* 5,000,000 years old.

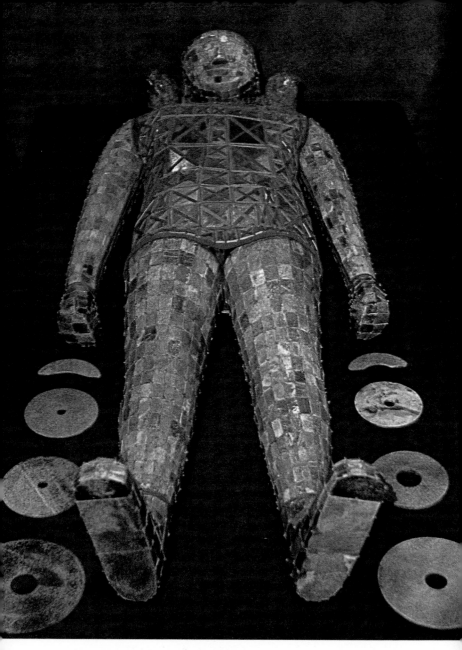

60 The jade burial suit of Princess Tou Wan, wife of Prince Liu Sheng of the Han dynasty.

61 An extremely fine glazed pottery figure of a horse of the Tang dynasty.

62 Chinese archaic bronze vessel of the early Chou dynasty.

63 Japanese wooden sculpture of a temple guardian. Kamakura period, 1185–1392.

64 Wooden sculpture of Bishamonten. Japanese, Kamakura period, 1185–1392.

65 A stone figure of a god from Teotihuacan, Mexico.

66 Mohica pottery stirrup vase. The Mohica culture in Peru lasted from A.D. 400–800

67 Pottery vessel from the Nicoya region of Nicaragua, c. A.D. 1,000–1,500

The interior of the megalithic temple of Mnaidra, Malta, showing several layers of the corbelled roof, c. 2300 B.C.

were simple structures, probably of a single chamber, but they soon became more complex with two or more chambers and transepts opening off a passageway. The basic plan common to all temples is a passage with branching pairs of transepts. Sometimes, because of alterations at later dates, this is extremely difficult to recognise. The chambers are walled with orthostats, large standing stones; the floors are of torba (a kind of cement made from pounded broken pottery), beaten and polished limestone powder, or occasionally limestone flags. Some temples have the transepts walled by large boulders in a more cyclopean technique, although the outer wall is composed of giant megalithic slabs. As with all Maltese temples, the space between the inner and outer wall is filled with earth and rubble. Some of the standing stones are extremely large and weigh many tons.

The most elaborate megalithic complex is to be found at Tarxien, where three buildings have been combined in a single outer wall to make a gigantic complex, the middle building having three pairs of chambers opening off a passage which terminates in a truncated chamber. These buildings are today known as 'temples'—a term first applied in the nineteenth century. They are characteristic of two main phases,

109

Ggantija (2700 B.C.), named after a temple site on the island of Gozo, and Tarxien (2300 B.C.).

The economic prosperity of Malta during this period must have reached its zenith, for to construct such massive stone buildings with simple stone tools and without sophisticated engineering tackle required a great deal of social organisation, apart from ingenuity. It also required economic freedom which indicates that by the third millennium B.C. man in Malta had developed his agrarian economy to an advanced state, probably due to the extremely favourable natural conditions. This allowed him not only to erect massive structures, but to spend time in decorating the interiors of many of them with fine relief carvings and sculptured figures of deities. Some of the designs of these reliefs are extremely intricate and must rank among the major artistic treasures of mankind.

The megalithic art may be divided into two parts, based on the medium in which they were executed—carvings, mainly in relief, and paintings. Most of the art is in the form of carvings, for only one site contains paintings, the unique underground Hypogeum of Hal Saflieni.

Many of the designs represented on the carved reliefs were also incised onto pottery. The pottery itself was extremely graceful and the shapes many and varied. Thousands of fragments were found in the temples, the remains of dedications and libations. The same motif inspiration can also be seen in the ochre paintings on the walls and ceilings of two chambers in the large underground temple and burial complex at the village of Hal Saflieni. This underground treasury has produced many pottery vessels and two interesting figurines of a sleeping lady or goddess on a couch. These unique figures have been interpreted as the oracle receiving her oracular revelations in a dream, while others have suggested that she may be dead and lying on a bier. While the former is possible, the latter is plausible as the remains of over seven thousand individuals were found in the chambers.

The sculptured reliefs are not the only unusual antiquities associated with the buildings; the numerous limestone figures of deities also deserve mention. There are at least two types. Most common is the figure of an obese lady often shown seated, one hand drawn across her stomach and the other resting on her knee, or, when she is standing, hanging by her side. The obesity of the figures contrasts strongly with the slimness of the idols of Cycladic Greece. Another figure is that which may be a man, perhaps a priest in the garments of the goddess. An interesting feature of these idols is that some have detachable heads.

Terracotta figure 'The Venus of Malta' from the pre-historic temple of Hagar Qim, Malta.

Marble figure of a woman, made in the Cycladic Islands, 2500–2000 B.C.

It is obvious from the material remains that great attention was paid to magico-religious matters, probably to ensure the fertility of the soil. Ironically, it is possible that these people's ignorance of agricultural science, along with the very act of erecting massive buildings with the vast amount of wood and soil that would be necessary for their construction and which probably contributed to a change in the fertility of the soil, may have led to the downfall of the culture. Something happened, for shortly after the erection of the last temples the culture appears to have suffered some natural calamity and declined. There then appears to have been an interval of some years before a new migration of men from Sicily. This time they were not in the Neolithic state, but had the use of bronze, and thus brought the Bronze Age to Malta.

After the megalithic age, a succession of different cultures left their imprint on Malta. The island is a virtual treasure house of antiquities of all periods—Bronze Age, Iron Age, Phoenician, Greek, Roman, Islamic and Norman. The fact that Malta is so rich archaeologically has led men to search for antiquities on the island from the earliest times. Collections were made with little or no record being kept of where they came from. An exception was Fra. G. Francisco Abela who made one of the most famous collections in the middle of the seventeenth century. He was Vice-Chancellor of the Order of the Knights of St John, and he used the information from his collection to write a *History of Malta* in 1647. Today, most of the archaeological treasures of all periods are housed in the National Museum, but the damage caused by the uncontrolled treasure hunting of early years will be forever felt.

10
Greece

Greece has traditionally been looked upon as the cradle of Western civilization. The grandeur and sophistication of ancient Greece is epitomised by superb marble sculptures, and painted black and red figured pottery, housed in many museums throughout the world, as well as numerous superb buildings, the ruins of which are dotted throughout the Greek countryside. The home of both classical and modern philosophical and political thought, its history is, however, far older than these antiquities. For it was the home of earlier cultures that have left behind a heritage as valuable and important as the classical civilization.

The Neolithic cultures of the Peloponnese have only recently received the attention they deserve. Before the arrival of the Greeks, the country was populated by numerous tribes that developed and flourished in their own rather primitive ways. These early cultures, however, provided the background for the major cultural developments of later centuries. The development of these cultures was often linked with that of the Greek islands, especially Crete.

Prior to the discovery of Mycenae in 1874, the existence of a pre-Hellenic civilization had only been hinted at in the epic works of Homer and in some of the early chronicles. These stories had been taken by historians to be purely legendary. One man, Heinrich Schliemann, however, thought otherwise. He was convinced that the stories were based on fact, and set about a systematic search to find evidence. By 1870, he had discovered the site of Homer's Troy on the Asiatic shore of the Dardanelles. Encouraged by this success, he transferred his search to Greece and began to excavate at Mycenae. There he discovered a civilization as wonderful as any that developed in Greece during the great classical period. In 1876, he thought he had found the burial of Agamemnon, and after having recovered a superb gold burial mask, sent a telegram to the King of Greece proudly informing him of his discoveries in the tomb. What he did not know then was that the civilization that he had discovered was centuries older than the era of the Homeric epics, to which Agamemnon belonged.

Between 1880–90 there were heated exchanges between Greek archaeologists about the dates of the finds. No-one could give more than relative dates to the culture, and it was left to the great Egyptologist, Sir Flinders Petrie, to date them. In his excavations in Egypt, he had found Mycenaean objects in the same context as those dating to the periods of the pharaohs Amenophis III and Rameses VI (1400–1050 B.C.) and was therefore able to place them within these dates. This evidence was further supported by the discovery of Egyptian objects at Mycenae. Thus the archaeology of a well-known culture helped date what at that time was a mystery civilization.

The search for other aspects of pre-Hellenic culture was taken up by Sir Arthur Evans, not on the mainland, but at Knossos in Crete where in 1900 he discovered the now famous Minoan civilization. Since then, numerous discoveries have been made which have helped paint a vivid picture of the pre-Hellenic world, both on the mainland of Greece and the Greek islands. Earlier stages in its cultural history have since been discovered and it is now known that, on the mainland, Mycenaean civilization was only the final stage of a culture that began centuries earlier.

The Minoan culture of Crete which was dominant between the sixteenth and fifteenth centuries B.C. subsequently entered a brief period of co-existence with Mycenae until, in the fourteenth to thirteenth century B.C., Mycenae became supreme. The Mycenaeans took over where the Minoans had left off. They were great colonists and travellers, and remains of their settlements can be found at various parts of the Aegean, the Levant and Cyprus.

Homer said Mycenae was 'Rich in Gold' and the marvellous gold objects found in the shaft graves certainly tend to confirm this. Mycenaean gold work and jewellery is extremely fine, although it cannot compare with the earlier, more vibrant and vital Minoan work. Pottery was again greatly influenced by the traditions of Minoan Crete, the early items in particular being very similar. Designs varied and were quite ingenious, being mainly abstract representations of floral, animal and marine motifs, although some vessels are decorated with concentric bands and linear and curvilinear motifs, while others are decorated with stylised figures. There were numerous different shapes of vessels, some of which are extremely graceful. The surface was usually buff with the decoration in a brown slip.

Mycenaean architecture was extremely advanced, with large palaces, tombs and other elaborate buildings. Palace architecture was similar to

Cretan, and like some of the Cretan palaces some rooms were decorated with painted frescoes, though probably to a lesser extent than in Crete. Sculpture was also produced and a very few fine examples are known including the monumental sculpture of facing lions known as the Lion Gate at the entrance to the Citadel of Mycenae, and the fine funerary stelae of a chariot scene from shaft grave V, of grave circle A, also at Mycenae.

Recent research suggests that there was cultural continuity from the Mycenaean period to the classical period. Evidence of this can be found in the Mycenaean Linear B clay tablets which have been deciphered by Michael Ventris and John Chadwick. Contrary to what scholars expected they were found to be written not in a pre-Hellenic language, but in Greek. The fact that some of the tablets have not been able to be read may suggest that non-Greek people may have co-existed with Greek-speaking people. Thus the tablets hint of a link between Greek-speaking and non-Greek-speaking peoples—a link between cultures. After the decline of the Mycenaean civilization, there was a period of some four to five hundred years, during which the basis for the great Greek classical civilization was laid down.

The pottery that followed that of the Mycenaean era was notably different, the designs being formalised and geometric. These gradually became more relaxed to include abstract representations of animals and people, until the introduction of Attic black-figured pottery in the sixth to fifth century B.C. Sculpture underwent similar developments.

The classical period was truly the golden age of Greece. It was a period of great artistic, philosophical and technological development. The philosophical and political ideas still affect us today, as does the influence of Greek architecture and art.

Greek classical pottery is probably the finest the world has ever seen. The pottery one commonly sees in museums is Attic, from the state of Attica which was the city state of Athens. As it is today, so the pottery of Athens was even then famous throughout the ancient world. Its vessels had a fine black glaze and were often decorated with scenes of everyday life, the theatre, athletics, mythology, and funerary scenes. Apart from the plain vessels, the decoration was also carried out in either black-figure or red-figure and additional colours such as purple and white were sometimes used. Black-figured decoration is earlier than red-figured; its use lasted for about one hundred and fifty years from 600 B.C. to 450 B.C. Red-figure was in use roughly between 530–300 B.C.

In black-figured decoration, the figures were marked in black on a

116

Greek Attic black-figured amphora showing Achilles slaying Penthesilea, queen of the Amazons. 540–530 B.C.

Greek bronze figure of Aphrodite, probably 3rd century B.C.

buff or terracotta background. Sometimes pots are found in reverse, that is, in black with details incised onto the pot. Red-figure decoration was virtually the negative of black-figure, the pot being covered in a black glaze with the exception of the figure or design which was left buff. Details were then painted in. A further type of Attic pottery was reserved purely for funerary use. These pots were decorated with painted figures on a white ground. In this case the figures might also be delicately coloured. The workmanship of these vessels was extremely fine (the labour being split between the potter and the painter).

It is difficult in a book of this size to single out objects and material remains of the Greek classical culture for discussion as there is so much of merit. The architecture is well known as is the sculpture. Classical Greece produced some of the greatest sculptors the world has ever seen. Their works were sought after by the Romans who copied them, using them as models and ideals for their own works. It was a status symbol for a Roman antiquary to own a piece of Greek statuary. Sculpture decorated temples and the major public buildings, but a lesser figurative art existed, that of the terracotta figurine. Numerous figures of terracotta have been recovered from various sites throughout Greece. Subjects are varied, and include seated figures of the goddess Athena, scenes of everyday life, actors etc. Later the art of terracotta modelling developed, and a type of figurine evolved which we call Tanagra after a cemetery in Boeotia, where a large number were found. The Tanagra style was not restricted to the terracotta figures, but was also used for sculpture, and it is possible that the style so freely used in clay was originally sculptural. The Romans copied it freely, even to the point of placing commissioned portrait heads on Tanagra bodies! Realism is the keynote to the style. These terracottas are, of course, a lesser art, often being mass produced. On the other hand the bronze sculptures were on a par with fine marble sculptures and, from the technological point of view, even surpassed them.

Greece has attracted the scholar and the archaeologist from the earliest times and there is little doubt that she will continue to inspire generations of archaeologists to look deeper into her past, for the education and delight of future generations.

11
The Greek Colonies

The growth of population in Greece was accompanied by an increased demand for food. The area of fertile land could not provide sufficient food for the population, a fact that stimulated the colonization of neighbouring lands. Besides reducing the population of Greece itself, the colonies helped by trading goods which were not available on the mainland.

The Greek city-states founded colonies in southern Italy and Sicily, at various places in the Aegean and the Mediterranean sea and on the coast of Asia Minor. There were a number of Greek settlements along the coast of Asia Minor, but perhaps the most important was on the island of Rhodes. Pottery made here is known as 'East Greek'. Here, around the first quarter of the seventh century B.C., the geometric style of decoration gave way to a style of painting which included animal friezes and lotus flowers. Meander and cable patterns were subsidiary. The wild goat is the most common animal depicted and because of this it is sometimes known as the 'wild goat' style. The technique was extremely free and somewhat careless; designs were painted in dark brown, purple and white on a rather coarse and gritty clay body. Later, at the end of the seventh century, 'black-figure' pottery was introduced.

The Greeks ventured westward to Italy when, during the eighth and seventh centuries, they colonised both the south east and south west coasts. These colonies prospered and by the beginning of the fourth century B.C. the wealth and prosperity of their cities could be compared with that of Athens and Corinth. The first city to be built was at Cumae, a colony of Charus, in about 750 B.C. Cumae is north of Naples and it is possible that Ischia, an island in the bay of Naples, was the first great settlement. Further settlements were made on Sicily. Here on the eastern shore near the Strait of Messina was founded Naxos, a city that was destroyed in 403 B.C. Other cities were built to guard the passage through the Strait of Messina—these included Zarcle (Messina) and Rhegium (Reggio). Syracuse was also settled and later became a large and important city. On the mainland the notorious city of Sybaris was founded about the year 720 B.C.

The Greeks travelled far and wide; they established settlements on the coast of southern France at Marseilles c. 600 B.C., and on the southern coast of Spain. In north Africa, they founded cities along the shores of Libya and even founded the city of Naucratis at the mouth of the Nile, the great centre of Greco-Egyptian cultural relations about the year 650 B.C. There was no unified central government and each city was a self controlled city state with its own ruler. This often created inter-city rivalry, frequently with bloody results—more Greeks fought each other than any foreign foe. The settlers of these colonies were completely independent, and owed no allegiance to their homeland, although there were often sentimental ties.

The colonies created enormous trade with Greece, exporting raw materials, metal ores, wood, etc., as well as foodstuffs such as wheat, wine and cattle. In return, they imported a variety of goods including 'Attic' pottery which was greatly treasured. With the decline of vase painting in Greece, local South Italian potteries blossomed, at first producing vessels in the Attic tradition. By the fourth century, however, this influence had declined and had been replaced by a fine local tradition. The style, which is freer than that of Attic pottery, is basically 'red-figure' ware; in other words, the opposite to the 'black-figure'. It was extremely ornate being enhanced with secondary colours such as purple, white and yellow. The surface of the pottery does not have the sheen of that of the Greek homeland.

South Italian pottery can be divided into four main types. The most ornate is the Apulian ware; its shapes are elaborate and its colours vibrant. Lucanian pottery is more restrained; the designs are more formal and stiffer with little secondary colour. Campanian ware, on the other hand, is more colourful. Paestan pottery is distinguishable by the fact that figures are usually painted on each side of the vessel and included within a square panel of volutes or palmettes. A separate Sicilian ware has also been distinguished. One of the finest and most comprehensive collections of South Italian Greek pottery outside Italy is in the British Museum, London.

During the eighteenth and nineteenth centuries, large numbers of red-figured vases were collected for their artistic qualities alone. Huge quantities were dug up and sold to antiquaries. Today, this is still a problem. In spite of efforts by the authorities to halt the trade, large numbers of vases and other objects are being unearthed every year in unauthorised excavations by the 'clandestini' antiquity dealers.

121

In recent years, the most adventurous archaeological expedition in south Italy has been the search for the lost city of Sybaris. The eight year search was initiated by an American named Orville Bullitt. In 510 B.C. the first city of Sybaris was destroyed by the neighbouring city of Croton, but was later rebuilt on another site. The destruction of Sybaris was instantaneous. Bullitt believed that because of this, if the city could be found, it would prove as interesting as that of Pompeii. The problem was to find a city of no more than two square miles (5.18 sq km). An additional problem was that there was every likelihood that it would be buried deeply, probably more than twenty feet (6 m) down. Collaborating in the search was Froelich G. Rainey, the Director of the Museum of the University of Pennsylvania. Included in the team was Signor Lerici, an Italian who had developed special instruments for locating subterranean Etruscan tombs. Also with them was a representative from a firm of instrument manufacturers in Oxford. The plan was to use every available scientific aid, for without them there seemed little chance of success. In charge of the scientific equipment was Elizabeth Relph, Associate Director of the Applied Science Centre for Archaeology at the University of Pennsylvania. After studying the area with scientific instruments, a specially designed drill was employed to collect cores of soil samples. After years of search and many disappointments, in December 1968, the site was discovered and one of the greatest archaeological finds made. To the layman, however, it was not spectacular in the material aspect, as some other excavations were, as the remains could not be laid completely bare because of their great depth.

Other South Italian Greek colonies have been found, whose remains are far more colourful and attractive. The search for Sybaris, however, is really an illustration of modern archaeology using the latest scientific aids, to add to our knowledge of the past, rather than a treasure hunt for antiquities.

12
The Roman Empire

The antiquities of the Romans have long attracted the attention of the antiquaries. Roman sculpture was greatly sought after during the Italian Renaissance, the fifteenth and sixteenth centuries, just as the Romans themselves collected Greek sculpture as a symbol of status.

The Romans can perhaps be described as the greatest civilizing force ever known. The history of Rome is to a great degree a history of a large part of the ancient world, for her civilizing influence was felt over a wide area. The history of Rome is also a history of her army, for on it depended her wealth and empire.

The Romans created one of the greatest empires the world has ever seen. Their expansionist policies brought them control of a large part of the ancient world. Roman imperialism was, however, different from many of the later attempts at empire building. It was a great civilizing influence especially in the west. Although it conquered by force, it Romanised as it went, with the conquered eventually helping to conquer others. It was this policy of assimilation that enabled a city state to rule over such a large area.

Excavations have given us a huge amount of information on the origin and growth of the Roman Empire. Excavations in Rome itself have revealed large parts of the Forum, the Colosseum built by the Roman Emperor Vespasian (70–79 A.D.) and his son Titus (79–81 A.D.), market-places, baths, temples etc., while outside Rome numerous tombs, villas and roads help to paint a picture of Roman Italy. The most spectacular excavations have been at Pompeii and Herculaneum in the south of Italy, near Naples. Here in 79 A.D. two prosperous cities were destroyed and evidence of their way of life preserved by the lava and ashes from the volcano Vesuvius. Excavation has been able to give us a superb picture of life in a provincial city. The business quarter, with its bakers and wine shops, places of entertainment, brothels, theatre, the official area and the houses, has all been faithfully preserved. Along some of the roads it is even possible to see the grooves cut into the stone flags by the wheels of carts and chariots. Not all Roman archaeology is like this, however, for in the west, outside Italy, where there were no great cities before the Romans, the most common Roman remains are those of the legionary fortresses and farming villas. Where there were Roman cities, they were modelled on the capital, with amphitheatres and temples, etc. Roman towns have been excavated, but their remains are naturally less rich than those of the capital. In Britain, knowledge of Roman towns has been gained from Colchester (Camulodunum) and excavations at many other sites including Verulamium (near St. Albans), Wroxeter, Winchester (Venta Belgarum) and London (Londinium).

Eastwards the Romans built on already existing civilizations and the remains of the Roman period are far more impressive than in the West.

But just who were the Romans? Why did they develop and expand to such an extent? These are important questions that perhaps we should ask ourselves—the answer is fascinating. Rome grew from a small city-state dominated by the Etruscans. It shook off Etruscan control and eventually controlled areas of Italy originally under Etruscan domination. The formative centuries were bloody with internal disorders between the patricians or aristocracy and the plebeians or ordinary citizens who were seeking a form of democracy, and with other members of Italic Italy who were seeking the benefits of Roman citizenship. At the same time Rome had to defend herself against barbarian attacks and the expansionist policy of Carthage. It was a difficult period, but she emerged dominant with a strong military arm and a political structure which made her supreme in the ancient world. It was her citizen army, formed originally by the necessity for self defence, which enabled her to influence the development of many countries.

The birth of Rome as an imperialist power begins with the First Punic War in 264–241 B.C. Before then, her expansionism was mainly confined to Italy. With Rome's victory in the war and the declaration of peace in 241 B.C. she acquired her first province, Corsica and Sardinia. Hannibal, the Carthaginian general, launched the Second Punic War in 219 B.C. with his attack on the Greek colony of Saguntium, breaking a pact. Hannibal advanced almost unchecked, the Romans suffering a series of defeats. At the battle of Cannae in 216 B.C. the Romans are thought to have lost 50,000 men. The struggle was to rage for a number of years, until defeat came for the Carthaginians in 202 B.C. when Hannibal was defeated by Scipio at Zama. Rome was victorious and was now the major Mediterranean power. Carthaginian domination of the Iberian peninsula was replaced by Roman, and the newly acquired land was divided into two provinces in 197 B.C.—Hispania Citerior and Hispania

Ulterior.

For a time Carthage held on to her territory in Africa, but after the Third Punic War (150-146 B.C.), the power of Carthage was destroyed and her territories became the Roman province of Africa. Rome had been forced into the area of Cisalpine Gaul during the First and Second Punic Wars and it became a province in 181 B.C. Attacks by the Ligurian tribes on Rome's old ally Massilia (Marseilles) caused her to establish another province, Gallia Narbonensis or Provincia (Provence), an area on both sides of the Rhône, which extended roughly from the Pyrénées to the Maritime Alps.

Originally Rome had no territorial ambitions in the east. She had been forced a number of times into various conflicts, but after victory had withdrawn her troops or established a protectorate. After the Third Macedonian War (171-167 B.C.) in which the ruler, Perseus, was defeated and brought as a prisoner to Rome, Rome was again forced to intervene when Andriscus attempted to resuscitate the monarchy.

Macedonia became a Roman province in 146 B.C. and was enlarged to include the whole country up to the borders of Macedonia and Epirus after war with the Achaeans and their defeat at Corinth in 146 B.C. The province of Asia was bequeathed to the Romans after the death of Attalus, the last king of Pergamum. Other provinces were added, Cyrene in 74 B.C., Bithynia and Crete in 67 B.C., Pontus in 65 B.C., Cilicia in 65 B.C. (originally constituted in 102 B.C.), Syria in 64 B.C. and Cyprus in 58 B.C. In 55-54 B.C. Julius Caesar raided Britain in order to prevent it being used as a sanctuary for rebels who were creating trouble in Gaul, which he had conquered. It was not until 43 A.D., under the Emperor Claudius, that Britain was invaded and added to Rome's territories.

All was not quiet at home, however, where a number of political changes were being made, sometimes accompanied by bloodshed and civil war. Rome was in turmoil with the old rivalry between the plebeians and the patricians. Julius Caesar was assassinated in 44 B.C. His murderers were defeated at Philippi by his adopted son Octavian and Mark Antony. Another civil war broke out between Octavian and Antony after the latter married Cleopatra, and gave Roman provinces to her children. After the battle at Actium in 31 B.C. Cleopatra and Antony committed suicide. Octavian became the first Roman Emperor and ruled for forty-five years from 31 B.C. to 14 A.D. In 27 B.C. he acquired the title Augustus ('revered'). The empire was further extended during his reign.

Rome was a trading nation and her wares were traded throughout the

125

empire and beyond. Roman trading stations have been found as far afield as India, and Roman goods even found their way to China.

The antiquities of Rome are perhaps the best known of the ancient world. Museums in many countries exhibit typically Roman artefacts which may have been made locally. As well as commodities of produce, artefacts such as pottery and glass were traded extensively. The famous Roman shiny red pottery 'Terra Sigilata' or Samian ware was made in various centres in Gaul and traded throughout the Empire; local copies were also made. Glass was made in the glass-making centres of Syria and Egypt, where the craft had a long history, and later in the Rhineland. The evidence of Roman civilization is extensive. It lies above and below ground throughout the Roman empire. In spite of her military and political preoccupations, Rome produced great masters of art and architecture, whose output will forever rank among the wonders of the world.

A third-century A.D. *Roman bath-house, discovered under the A1 motorway, Hertfordshire, England. It has now been preserved.*

The empire continued until, under the strain of internal disorders and barbarian invasions, it began to break up. After the death of the Emperor Theodosius in 395 A.D. the empire was divided between his two sons, a division that was to be permanent. In A.D. 410 the Ligottis attacked and sacked Rome itself, and, although the imperial succession continued until A.D. 455 in the West, the imperial administration and institutions were to live on only in the East, in a modified form in Byzantium, 'the new Rome'. The old Roman Empire was dead.

13
Great Britain

The antiquities of Britain have long roused men's curiosity, and the first real attempt to understand the 'barbarian' past, or pre-Roman period, was made during the sixteenth century. The rise of nationalism stimulated scholars like Camden, who in 1586 published his *Britannia*, the first comprehensive topographical study of England. Interest in Britain's past increased during the following centuries with the Society of Antiquaries being founded in the early eighteenth century. Early societies such as this did much valuable work, especially in field-recording where they were still basically concerned with classical antiquities.

Throughout the eighteenth and nineteenth centuries, archaeology as a discipline was almost non-existent, although there were notable exceptions, such as John Aubrey and William Stukley, especially the latter whose meticulous observations are appreciated even today, but on the whole antiquaries remained more interested in objects than in their contexts, and archaeology at that time was just a glorified treasure hunt. This all changed at the end of the nineteenth century, when General Pitt-Rivers the father of modern archaeology, took the first steps by carrying out meticulous excavations at his estate on Cranborne Chase in Dorset. His scientific approach and monumental reports laid the basis for archaeological research in this country. Today the standards applied to archaeology in Britain are among the highest in the world. Both professionals and amateurs have a high standard and a scientific approach which gains international respect. There are, of course, some exceptions, and a few bad excavations are conducted, but the quality of the main body of the work shows them up.

Over the centuries Britain has played involuntary host to innumerable immigrants and invaders and within her shores can be found antiquities with connections with many parts of Europe and of many periods.

The Palaeolithic period, or Old Stone Age, is well represented and there are many thousands of stone implements in museums from various sites, some little known and others well known such as Swanscombe.

Lower Palaeolithic flint hand-axe from a 100 ft (30 m) gravel terrace of the Thames, Maidenhead.

129

These hand axes, ovates and other implements found on the gravel terraces are many thousands of years old and it would not be unusual to see a specimen in a museum labelled, 'Hand Axe, Acheulian, 250,000 years old'. Unlike Europe, there are no examples of Palaeolithic art like the paintings of Lascaux in France, or the little carved figure of the Venus of Willendorf. However, the flint implements themselves are evidence of the skill and craftsmanship of these early men and some can even be considered as works of art. The Palaeolithic period lasted for tens of thousands of years, until about 9000 B.C. when there was a change to the Mesolithic period, the Middle Stone Age. The Palaeolithic people were hunters. The Mesolithic people were food gatherers; they were still using stone tools, but the economy had changed. They were in an intermediate stage, between the Old Stone Age and the New Stone Age of the Neolithic people.

Some scholars have referred to the Neolithic period as the Neolithic revolution, for revolution it was, not a violent revolt, but a slow economic change of people switching from food gatherers to food producers, and becoming agriculturalists. This new state is represented in Britain by polished stone tools and other artefacts, and for the first time pottery, along with sites such as causewayed camps, a good example of which is Windmill Hill, Wiltshire, and long barrows or communal burials. Both these were earthen constructions of massive proportions. The long barrows were long mounds of earth which covered the remains of a number of individuals. Sometimes they had chambers constructed of large stones. These Megalithic structures are also found in other parts of Europe. To the Neolithic period, too, belongs the first phase of the construction of Stonehenge. The Aubrey Holes (named after the antiquary John Aubrey) and the ditch belong to this period. The Blue Stones and large Sarsen trilithons were constructed later during the Bronze age. Not far from Stonehenge is the banked enclosure of Avebury, which was also constructed during the Neolithic period.

Antiquities of this period can be found in museums throughout the country. Many of the economic changes were the result of the influx of immigrants from the Continent, and thus many antiquities bear strong resemblances to their European counterparts. A new migration from the Continent heralded the end of the Neolithic period, when a people using pottery beakers and knowing the use of bronze settled in Britain. Their 'Beaker' pottery is most distinctive; the common types are either bell-shaped or long-necked and decorated with impressed designs. The Bronze Age followed, and in comparison to Beaker pottery the pottery of that time is large and crude, and mainly consists of cinerary urns. There was little in the way of sophisticated or artistic artefacts, the exception being the Wessex Culture, which flowered for a short period, and which produced some fine gold ornaments etc., a number of which have been found in their burial mounds or barrows. Until recently the Wessex Culture chieftains were credited with relations with the Mycenaean culture, though present research now throws some doubt on this.

It was not until the Iron Age that objects which can in any way be described as sophisticated or artistic were made in any quantity. It was perhaps the peak of 'Barbarian' culture. Fine pots were produced, although until late in the Iron Age these were hand-thrown, and metalwork rose to great heights, not only in the production of everyday domestic objects, and items of personal ornament, but also in the superb trappings of war such as shields, helmets, swords and horse-trappings. The superb electrum Torc from Snettisham in Kent and the fine intricately engraved bronze mirror from Desborough in the Midlands both illustrate this well. Both items are in the British Museum. With the Roman Invasion of Britain in A.D. 43 a new cultural element was introduced—Romanitas, the Roman way of life. The native Britons either adopted this new culture wholesale or incorporated minor Roman details into their artefacts. Thus the antiquities of Roman Britain are either pure Roman or a curious mixture of Celtic and Roman.

The urban British were quickly Romanised, and within a few years of the invasion they began to adopt the Roman way of life. Villas with farms were established, roads built and towns founded. The buildings attempted a true Roman style, with mosaics and all the trappings of Roman civilization such as underfloor heating, and bath suites. At Aquae Sulis, present-day Bath, they built an elaborate series of baths, and temples were built at Colchester, London and other towns. However, there were areas where native resistance and hostility to the Romans existed, a fact clearly reflected in their native style of artefacts. Despite great armies of Roman soldiers, the conquest of upland Britain was never completed and the control of what is now England and Wales took nearly half a century. The south and east of the country had traded with conquered Gaul before the invasion, and within a few years of the invasion some tribes and cities began to adopt the Roman way of life. Roads were built and towns were founded. People in the towns and cities grew more aware, through trade, of the advantages of the Roman way of life. Britannia became a firmly established part of the Roman Empire.

Hoard of Roman coins from Dorchester, England.

The Romans who were posted to Britain imported for their own use beautifully potted vessels in red 'Samian ware' or Terra Sigilata, specialities of the provinces of the Empire, and glass vessels from Rome and Syria and, later, from the Rhineland. These have been found at many sites throughout Britain. The remains of Roman Britain are more plentiful in some areas of the country than others. Places like Rochdale in Lancashire have produced evidence of Roman occupation with antiquities such as a silver arm of victory, bracelets etc. being found. Colchester and the area around Hadrian's wall in Northumbria and Cumbria are very rich in Roman remains. Equally rich, but not necessarily in visible remains, is Dorchester in Dorset, with Maiden Castle nearby. Maiden Castle was the site of one of the bloodiest battles of the Roman invasion. It was fortified by members of the Durotrigian tribe, and held out against the Sixth Augusta Legion under the future Emperor Vespasian for a number of days before being overrun in an attack on the east gate of the hill fort. Three centuries later, a Roman temple was built on the site.

After the Romans left Britain, the country fell into chaos and anarchy prevailed, until the establishment of the Anglo-Saxon Kingdom. The Danes also invaded parts of England and established settlements on the east coast. The last people to conquer Britain were the Normans. Each culture has left its mark on the country, and in some areas of the country an archaeologist may excavate the remains of many cultures layer upon layer. Britain is so rich in archaeological remains that every day, through

132

modern development in towns and cities or modern agricultural methods in the country, some site or object is being destroyed. In an effort to save information from these sites as well as to preserve some of the objects, emergency excavations have been carried out, large and small, in a constant battle against time, to save as much of Britain's heritage for the future as possible. The task has proved greater than had been anticipated, and the bulldozers have been winning hands down. In an effort to combat this, archaeologists have got together to form 'Rescue', a charitable organisation to raise money for excavation and to organise things on a national basis. The future hope for Britain's past lies in organisations such as these, for unless something is done there will be little for the archaeologists of tomorrow to do.

Silver dish from the Mildenhall Treasure, 4th century A.D. *The outer frieze shows the triumph of Bacchus over Hercules. The central mask is of Neptune or Oceanus.*

14
India

The Indian sub-continent is a vast treasure house of history. As a geographical entity India is huge, not only a country, but almost a continent. Throughout history it has played host to many races of people over thousands of years, each of which has left its mark in some material aspect. The environment of the various regions of India has often been a very important factor in determining the development of cultures and the manner in which they advanced.

Although India's history began many thousands of years ago in the Palaeolithic period, the first elements of civilization were laid down on the western coast in the Valley of the Indus in the third millennium B.C. Here, along the banks of the great river and on the sea coast at Lothal, a civilization which has been likened to that of Sumer flourished between 2500–1700 B.C. It is only fair, however, to say that this comparison between the two cultures is only superficial, and in such a comparison the Indus civilization that developed along the banks of the Indus was of a very high standard, and far superior to anything that had preceded and even succeeded it.

The Indus culture was utilitarian in character and few antiquities of artistic merit have been found. There are, of course, exceptions and the exceptions in the Indus civilization are really worthy of note. Amongst these are the fine sculptured stone torsos, the stone busts of bearded men, and a magnificent small bronze statuette of a dancing girl. The latter is the earliest known bronze figure discovered in India. Found at Mohenjo Daro, in modern Pakistan, it is extremely plastic and full of the rhythm of life. The method used by the Indus craftsmen to make this figure continued to be used later during the classical Medieval periods, and is still used today—that of the Cire Perdue or 'lost wax' method.

Indian culture shares with that of China and Egypt a great national conservatism. This is evident even in a superficial examination of Indian art and culture. Indians have been a traditional conservative people. Although new ideas were introduced and accepted in India, the old traditions were not abandoned, but blended with the new. Even today in villages in various parts of the country, it is still possible to find terracotta figures similar in many respects to those made thousands of years ago.

The figure of the dancing girl from Mohenjo Daro is unique, for no other bronze figure of any significance has been found which pre-dates the Christian era.

The most famous of the Indus sculptures are the busts and heads of priest-kings or deities. Their similarity to the sculptures of eastern Syria and Mesopotamia makes them extremely interesting. They are not, however, identical, for unlike the sculptures of Mesopotamia they have beards, which the Indian sculptors carved as long straight grooves. The eyes too are rendered differently; they are carved as long thin almonds, contrasting strongly with the owl-like stare of the Mesopotamian types. The general air of the Indian busts is one of nobility and superiority.

Two realistically sculptured torsos, noticeably different in style from the heads, have been found at another Indus site, Harappa. Carved from grey and red stone, they are masterpieces in miniature. In many ways they resemble more the classical sculpture of later periods and may not, in fact, be contemporary with the other examples from the Indus Valley. In addition to the sculptures mentioned, numerous terracotta figurines were made in the shape of animals, toy carts and mother-goddesses. The goddesses were always modelled in a highly stylised fashion, and shown grotesquely overdressed and decked with jewellery. The terracotta figurines often show the strong sense of humour of the Indus artists.

The Indus Valley was not the only civilization which flourished at this time; there were others in various parts of India, both east and west, but perhaps the Indus civilization has left more physical remains than others, and is thereby able to capture the imagination of modern men. Another great difference with the other early Indian cultures is that the Indus civilization was literate. Numerous seals with enigmatic pictures and writing have been found which have been a challenge to archaeologists who have tried to decipher them, so far without success.

The next major event in Indian archaeology, after the decline of the Indus civilization, is the invasion of Afghanistan and north-west India by Alexander the Great. This invasion had an importance over and above a military campaign, for it marked the introduction into India of Hellenistic ideas. This Hellenistic influence can be seen clearly in the material culture of that part of India for centuries after Alexander's visit. Also of importance upon Indian life and culture was the effect of the Great Mauryan Empire under the Emperors Chandragupta and Ashoka. This too showed influences from outside, in this case Persia. Many of the sculptures of the early Mauryan period show very strong Persian influence and in fact many may well have been the work of immigrant Persian sculptors who came to India after the fall of the Achaemenid Empire. It was at this time too that another great force began to make itself felt—religion, in this case Buddhism. From this time on, religion is a major influence, whether Buddhist or Hindu.

The Emperor Ashoka erected great stone pillars which, although of Persepoliton type, were not meant to support buildings, but were intended to act as memorials to commemorate special events. The symbolism of Ashoka's pillars was entirely Buddhist. They show extremely fine workmanship, combined with a strength and volume reminiscent of Persian rather than Indian works and some scholars have even argued that they show more influence of the Hellenistic school than the Persian. The Perso-Hellenic sculptures, said the great archaeologist Sir John Marshall, were the work of Hellenistic craftsmen from Bactria. However, opinions differ and it is equally possible that they are the work of Indian sculptors under Perso-Hellenic influence.

The art of the Gandhara region of north-west India is noted for its pseudo-Hellenic style. Gandhara was the name applied to the region around Peshawar on the North West Frontier. The style originated there, though influenced originally from outside, spread to Baluchistan, Afghanistan and even Central Asia. Gandhara itself had come under a number of influences and in 327 B.C. it was part of the Achaemenian Empire which was conquered by Alexander the Great. During the Mauryan empire it was consolidated with the rest of the Empire. It was later conquered by the Bactrian Kingdom which at that time, although cut off from Greece, had preserved an Hellenic culture. In the first century B.C. it was conquered by the Kushans, who ruled it until the White Huns overran north India in the fifth century A.D. Sculpture from this area mirrors these influences.

Basically, however, the sculptures of Gandhara express indigenous Buddhist ideas in a pseudo-Hellenistic style or, more correctly, Romano-Buddhist style as many of the Hellenistic ideals had been Romanised before they influenced the Indian sculptors. Some of the finest works of art of this exciting period have come from the great Gandhara city of Taxila in Sind.

India has so many archaeological sites where the remains of different eras have been preserved; north, south, east or west, the country is a living museum. Some of its history lies preserved in large mounds of earth, sites of old universities, cities, towns, or temples, while other aspects may be clearly visible—for example, buildings, temples or palaces, or natural features such as cliffs, which have been carved and made into temples. The art and culture of India is boundless.

Sandstone sculpture of a Yakshi or tree spirit. From a Jain stupa at Mathura, northern India, Kushan dynasty, 2nd century A.D.

137

In a survey such as this a few really important sites must be mentioned, all of which have played an important part in the history of this vast sub-continent. In Central India is the great site of Bharut, with its buildings and sculpture carved in low relief; the influence here is Buddhist. Another site in Central India, the ancient town of Mathura, has produced masterpieces of Gupta Buddhist sculpture while the site of Pataliputra, in eastern India, has preserved remains of Ashoka's empire. South-east, in Orissa, numerous antiquities of all periods are preserved. Also in the east, the medieval remains of the Pala period can be seen scattered over a wide area. The great cave temples of western India, such as Ellora and Ajanta, have preserved great sculptures and paintings in and on the living rock. At Ajanta are some of the finest Buddhist paintings in the whole of Asia.

In the south of India there are numerous architectural remains of all periods, mainly temples. The south was a great centre of bronze sculpture during the twelfth and thirteenth centuries and many have been preserved in the soil and buildings as well as in temples. At Amaravati numerous Buddhist remains dating to the first century A.D. have been found, while at Arikemedu the presence of a Roman trading station has been noted. Architecture, sculpture, bronzes, pottery; all have been preserved in their thousands.

These remains, really too numerous to mention, will pose problems and provide answers for archaeologists for years to come. Archaeology in India may yet hold many surprises.

15
China

China—the birthplace of invention! To many, the unfamiliar relics, shapes and art forms of the Orient are difficult to understand. However, beneath the unfamiliar façade we find the same face of civilization that is evident in the ancient cultures of the west and the New World. In fact, China was one of the greatest centres of civilization the world has ever known. Its influence was felt throughout the Far East, including Tibet and India.

Chinese history began in the Old Stone Age, the Palaeolithic period, but its history as a civilized culture began many thousands of years later, in Neolithic times. This massive country received immigrants and invasions from many of the surrounding lands, but it is interesting to note that they very quickly became assimilated into the indigenous Chinese culture, becoming completely Sinocised, in much the same way as Ancient Egypt assimilated non-Egyptian peoples and ideas, and moulded them in her own image.

However, as well as influencing others, China was herself influenced, both by other countries and by religious and philosophical ideas, though occasionally they were synonymous. China owes a great deal to India, both for artistic inspiration and religious stimulus. Buddhism was imported into China from India, but in the early days had to contend with strong competition from the indigenous religions of Taoism and Confucianism. Later, however, all three religions existed together in a sort of harmony, each in its way contributing to the development of Chinese culture.

One of the difficulties in studying the early periods of Chinese history is the lack of information from scientifically conducted excavations. Excavations in China have in the past been conducted in an extremely superficial and haphazard manner. There have been innumerable clandestine excavations by antique dealers and antiquaries seeking to enrich their purse rather than their minds. The result has been a wealth of antiquities (these can be seen enriching museums and private collections throughout the world) and a dearth of information. This unhappy

The central chamber of the tomb of Prince Liu Sheng of Chungshan of the Western Han dynasty, 206 B.C.–A.D. 24. Discovered in 1968.

situation has fortunately begun to change, and the Chinese government is now sponsoring and encouraging scientific research and the publication of new scientific information. However, there are so many questions to answer that it will be a long time before sufficient information is available to help us close the gaps in our knowledge.

Any appreciation of the material remains of Chinese culture must start with an examination of the fine Neolithic painted pots of the Yang Shao culture that flourished in the basin of the Yellow River. This culture produced extremely fine vessels, decorated with superb curvilinear designs. Strangely, in some respects they recall the vessels from the early civilizations of the Western hemisphere. Fine ritual jades were also made during this period.

The period of Chinese civilization most commonly illustrated by museum collections is the Bronze Age, the Shang (1523–1027 B.C.) and the Chou (1027–221 B.C.) dynasties. During this period a highly-organised and sophisticated civilization flourished in China during which works of great artistic merit and technological skill were produced. The Chinese have been credited with numerous inventions, and it is in the Shang dynasty that one can see this technological superiority demonstrated by the superb bronze casting of the Chinese artisan. During this time, as in later China, the worship of ancestors was popular and many bronze vessels were cast for use in the rituals and sacrifices connected with it. Other vessels were made to be used as funerary furniture, and buried with royalty, nobility and wealthy commoners. There are a number of different shapes each one used for a specific purpose.

Over the last fifty years hundreds of bronze vessels, dating to the Shang and Chou dynasties, have been excavated from tombs and burials in the area of the great Shang and Chou cities. These bronzes are magnificent works of art and are highly treasured. The Chinese themselves have always admired and venerated these ancient bronzes since early times, and in the Sung dynasty (A.D. 960–1280) scholars made the first serious attempt at a catalogue of their types.

Part of the mystique of these vessels is enveloped in the technological inventiveness of the Chinese craftsmen, for the techniques employed to produce these vessels are remarkable. Two processes were used, but the technique generally used was the Cire Perdue or 'lost wax' process. In this method an original was made by modelling the proposed shape of the interior of the vessel on a core of clay and other ingredients. On to this several layers of beeswax were added until the required shape of the vessel was achieved. The surface was carved with a highly stylised design of animals, dragons, masks, or geometric forms. Once the shape and design of the vessel had been completed it was covered with clay, thin at first and then afterwards thick, until a mould had been formed. Stays were inserted into selected points to hold the core in position with the outer mould, and a hole made to allow hot gases to escape when the mould was heated. Heating continued until all the wax had melted and evaporated, then molten bronze was poured in. After the mould had cooled it was broken open and the newly-cast bronze vessel removed to the finishing shop where workmen would remove all traces of casting. The early bronze workers were extremely clever, for stays were so arranged so any casting marks would be incorporated into the design. There were variations on this method; for instance it was possible to cast the wax original from a pottery mould. Some vessels were even made directly from pottery moulds. Artefacts other than bronze vessels were made during this exciting period of technological innovation, but it is the vessels which have caught the imagination of modern observers.

During the succeeding Han dynasty (206 B.C.–220 A.D.) ritual bronzes continued to be made, although much of the early originality had been lost. Other influences were making themselves felt in art, especially the barbarism of the Steppe nomads. With the artistic influence of the Steppes came a tendency to increased naturalism. This can clearly be seen, although sometimes it is accentuated and embellished with stylised motifs. In spite of this, animal and human figures, when portrayed, are instantly recognisable. It may even be, as some scholars have suggested, that the Steppe nomads introduced the mirror into China, after having taken the idea from the Greeks from the area around the Black Sea in about the fifth century B.C. This is, however, highly questionable, as mirrors have been found in Shang tombs near Anyang and it seems that this interesting, but doubtful, idea is wishful thinking, the Chinese having invented the mirror independently.

Numerous antiquities have been recovered from Han tombs and a clear insight into life at the time can be reconstructed by an examination of the technological and artistic standard of the remains, which is truly remarkable. Pottery, for instance, had progressed to such a state that, as early as the second century B.C., the Chinese were producing glazed pottery vessels and tomb figures. The Han tombs have also preserved some of the earliest lacquer-ware. Recently, one of the greatest masterpieces of Chinese bronze casting was discovered in a tomb of a provincial governor—the Flying Horse of Kansu. Another remarkable treasure of the period was the discovery of two complete jade funerary suits, from the adjoining tombs of Prince Liu Sheng of Chungshan and his wife, Princess Ton Wan.

In addition to these great masterpieces, much information about everyday life can be gleaned from sculpture which, during the Han dynasty, were generally bas-reliefs. Those that have survived are extremely interesting and help provide a visual idea of the everyday life of the period. The subjects are nearly always mythological or historical, but are depicted in contemporary settings. A large number of reliefs were found in the Wu Liang Tombs, in Shangtung.

The general style of Han reliefs, which are very flat, points to the fact that they may be carvings on stone of contemporary paintings. This is particularly helpful as it gives us an idea of the appearance of paintings which disappeared a long time ago.

There are few sculptures in the round, perhaps the most notable being the massive statues of horses, carved from boulders, at the tomb of General Ho Ch'u-Ping in the valley of the Wei River in Shensi; they date to about the second century B.C.

The break up of the Han dynasty brought with it chaos and poverty. People clung eagerly to the new religion, Buddhism, which had been introduced into China from India, and through which they felt they could achieve stability and peace. From the Six Dynasties period (280 A.D.–589 A.D.) onwards, religion became a major influence in artistic and cultural works. Paintings, sculpture in stone and bronze, and buildings were produced in increasing numbers. Buddhist images were commissioned both for worship in private and to be installed in temples. Buddhist bronzes of this early period are extremely rare, but literary sources assure us that they were produced and it is probable that imported images from the Gandhara region of north-west India and from Central Asia acted as models for the first Chinese images.

As with other civilizations of the ancient world, some of the most interesting finds have been made in ancient tombs. In China, a vast quantity of tomb figures has been found in burials of the Han (206 B.C.–220 A.D.) and T'ang (618–907 A.D.) periods. These fantastic figures are not rigid, but extremely plastic, and depict all manner of subjects of everyday life, and humans and animals. Those of the T'ang dynasty clearly reflect the cosmopolitan attitude of the time. Some depict foreigners, sometimes bearded, from the Near and Middle East, and Central Asia. Certainly the most famous are the marvellous figures of horses and camels, intended to accompany the deceased for use in the next world; these can be seen in museums all over the world. They are often treated as art objects, and it is important to remember that they were not intended as such, but are in fact archaeological evidence which help us to understand the social and cultural history of the time. These magnificent statues of horses are among the masterpieces of ancient China, and the vitality with which they have been executed rivals the great work of the classical Greek sculptors. Some of the models and figures are glazed, while others are simply painted with unfired pigments.

Chinese culture is continuous in spite of invasions by 'barbarians' and migrations of people from nearby lands; and this continuity is clearly shown in her antiquities. The conservative nature of her people has helped produce one of the longest lasting civilizations the world has ever seen. It is therefore unfortunate that our knowledge of such a civilization should be based on the few excavations that have taken place, literary evidence, and the slender information that can be gleaned from excavated objects divorced from their surroundings.

Thankfully this has now begun to change. The Chinese government is actively encouraging the scientific investigation of the country's remote history and perhaps in the not too distant future our knowledge of this fascinating part of the world will be enlarged by many more scientifically conducted excavations. Meanwhile, the superb artistic objects from the many periods of Chinese civilization will continue to attract the curiosity of those throughout the world who visit museums.

16
Japan

The antiquity of Japan has only recently attracted the research it so rightly deserves. The history of the classical periods has long been known, but even this has been able to be enlarged and corrected. Japan's history begins early in the Palaeolithic, but her history as a civilized culture does not begin until the Jomon period, the Neolithic.

Pottery made its appearance at an early date in Japan and developed in a curious manner, as can be seen in the unusual shapes of the Jomon pottery. The vessels were not made on a wheel, but formed by hand. Jomon means 'cord impressed', and this aptly describes the exterior of the vessels which were richly decorated with fantastic designs. The shapes are distinctive, but their appearance, although exciting, is not one of quality ceramically speaking, especially when they are compared with the vessels of high quality which were being produced in Bronze Age, Shang Dynasty China. The clay was rough with many impurities, and it was fired at a low temperature, but this lack of quality is made up for by the vigour and imagination of the shapes and decoration.

Pottery cult-figures began to be made by the Middle Jomon period, in about the tenth century B.C. They are almost always female and suggest a use in fertility worship. There are different types; some are small and almost animal like, others are quite heavy with a great deal of surface decoration. Unfortunately, we have little idea as to the religious practice or purpose for which they were intended.

In the third century B.C. a new people arrived in Kyushu, one of the outer islands of Japan. They were Mongoloid, probably from south China or even Indo-China, and they brought with them the influence of mainland China, gradually driving out the earlier inhabitants and occupying the main island of Japan, Honshu. This took many centuries. We call their culture Yayoi, after the site where it was first discovered. Their arrival in Japan marked the arrival of the Bronze and Iron Age simultaneously, for they brought the use of both metals with them. Thus, Japan missed a true Bronze Age and suddenly found herself in the Iron Age.

Early Japanese pottery vessel of the Jomon period 1000–2000 B.C.

Chinese influence during this period is very strong and can clearly be detected in many Japanese bronzes. However, the Japanese did not always copy, but developed many original designs and objects of their own. An unusual type of bronze 'bell', the Dotaku, first makes its appearance in the late Yayoi period. These are unlikely to have been used for any acoustic purpose and appear to have had some ritual use.

The peculiar shapes of Jomon pottery disappear in the Yayoi period with the introduction of the potters' wheel. Yayoi pottery has the normal symmetrical shapes one usually associates with the wheel. Pedestal-stemmed vessels are known, and many of the pots have vigorous stylised paintings.

Periods in Japan tend to overlap. The Yayoi culture lasted to about 500 A.D., but earlier in the fourth century A.D. the Old Tomb period had begun. This period is characterised by massive earthen tumuli surrounded by moats. These tombs have for long been taboo to the Japanese, a fact which has helped preserve the objects within them for present-day archaeologists. Fine objects of great beauty in stone, bronze, iron and even glass have been preserved in the tombs. The largest was constructed for the Emperor Nintoku who died in about 400 A.D. It occupies about eighty acres of land near Osaka.

With the Old Tomb period, we see the introduction of two ceramic innovations. Pottery becomes finer, better fired, and non-porous. Some objects show traces of a wood ash glaze and the influence of Korean potters can clearly be seen.

The other ceramic innovation is massive by comparison. The Haniwa figure developed from the practice of placing pottery cylinders, filled with earth and set closely together, around the massive mounds of earth of the tomb. They acted as a sort of buttress, to hold up the soil around the edges of the mound. With the passage of time, attempts were made to ornament these cylinders. They took on the form of humans and animals, inspired perhaps by the tomb figures of Han and Six Dynasties China, although they are completely different, being quite abstract and sophisticated and very pleasing to the modern eye. Inanimate objects were also modelled on the cylinders, with subjects such as armour, weapons, thrones etc. predominating. As pieces of sculpture, Haniwa figures are fascinating, as the ornamented plastic forms of the models contrast strongly with the stiff, inanimate cylinder beneath. Large numbers were made in an infinite variety of forms.

The basic shape of the Haniwa allowed both geometrical and abstract treatment of the subject. Facial features, such as noses and ears, were

147

modelled separately and attached, while the eyes and mouth were cut out of the clay. The effect was surrealist, like a science fiction creature. Although stylised, the details of costume etc. are extremely accurate and provide us with a valuable source of information on contemporary costume and material culture. Large numbers of Haniwa figures were made, for one tomb alone, that of the Emperor Nintoku in Izumo Province, had over eleven thousand.

There are a number of stories about the origin of the Haniwa, but most seem to be fictional, even that related in the Nihon Shaki, a sacred book of the eighteenth century. In it the story is told that the Haniwa were made as substitutes for human sacrifices at burial rites, like the original Chinese tomb figures. This seems unlikely as they were placed not inside but outside the tomb and, as we have seen, it is also possible to trace the Haniwa back to its utilitarian origins as simple pottery cylinders. No evidence of sacrifices such as seen in the Shang tombs of China has been found in Japan. It seems probable that the legend of the origin of Haniwa figures may have started by the very appearance of the figures, half buried as they were around the mound.

The whole direction of Japanese culture alters with the introduction of Buddhism in the sixth century A.D. As an influence on Japanese art and culture it was all powerful, bringing Japan in touch and under the influence of China and Korea from time to time.

The first Buddhist images appear to have been brought to Japan by the Buddhist mission from Korea in 552 A.D., although the first representation of the Buddha appears to be on a Chinese bronze mirror, dating to the first half of the third century, found near Nara. Other records relate that an artist versed in the making of images arrived in Japan from Korea in 557 A.D. By 604 A.D., Buddhism had become firmly established and received state recognition. From here onwards, Japanese culture passes out of the realm of archaeology and into that of history, though even then archaeology has a part to play.

17
Middle America

The Beginnings

When the Spanish Conquistador Hernando Cortés destroyed the great Empire of the Aztec in 1519, he had no idea of the vast antiquity of their ancestors and predecessors who had occupied the valley of Mexico for centuries. To him the Aztecs were pagan savages. But he was greatly mistaken for their culture was in many ways superior to that of Cortés' own. Even some of the soldiers who accompanied him had recognised that there was something more to these people than primitive savages. One of them, Bernal Diaz de Castillo, wrote 'We were astonished, and declared that this was like the wonders related in the Book of Amadis, on account of the huge towers, pyramids and the other buildings, all of stone, that rose above the water. Some of us soldiers even asked ourselves whether all we saw might not be a dream'.

Mexico's long history begins not in Mexico, but in the very north of the American continent, in Alaska, when, about 50,000 years ago, immigrants crossed from Asia to America, across a land bridge. The sea at that time was frozen and the land lower by some two hundred feet (60 m). Later, when the ice melted, it flooded the land and immigrants like the Navaho Indians had to cross to the New World in boats.

Mexico is part of Meso America, an area which extends south from the Soto La Marina River in Tamaulipas to the Motogua River in Honduras and the Gulf of Nioya in Costa Rica. Within this area numerous cultures developed at different periods in time. Over the centuries it has played host to a vast cultural spectrum, including among others the Olmecs, Teotihuacanos, Toltecs, Aztecs, Totonacs, Zapotecs, Mixtecs and Maya. Each culture has left behind antiquities testifying to its existence and providing clues to its history, its development and decline.

One of the oldest surviving antiquities of Meso America is the head of a Coyote or similar beast. Carved from part of a fossil vertebra of an extinct species of llama, it is thought to date to about 12,000 B.C. The men who carved it belonged to a group of nomadic hunters, who occupied the area around the shores of the lakes in the Valley of Mexico, hunting mammoth and other animals. These hunters were followed by food gatherers and, soon after, the first experiments in agriculture followed. By about 2500 B.C. villages had sprung up, agriculture had advanced, technology had improved in the production of stone tools, pottery began to be made, and crafts such as basketry and weaving flourished. Combined with this was a renaissance of religious thought which gave rise to a cult of the dead. During the Preclassic period, development continued and technology and the arts flourished, a form of hieroglyphic writing was invented, and a calendar. The Preclassic period can be divided into three, the Lower Preclassic (1700–1300 B.C.), Middle Preclassic (1300–800 B.C.), and the Upper Preclassic (800–200 B.C.) and major developments and advances took place during this period.

By the following Protoclassic period (200 B.C.–200 A.D.), the basis of the great civilizations of the Maya, Zapotec, and even Teotihuacan, had already been laid down and was clearly recognisable.

The Olmec civilization is the oldest of Mexico. Although there are large numbers of antiquities that can be labelled 'Olmec' little is known about the people themselves, and even the date of their culture is controversial. However, radiocarbon dating has placed it in the Middle Classic Period, about 800–400 B.C. To the untrained eye, the material remains of Meso America look much alike, but they are each different, each distinguishable by their own artistic trade mark. Olmec art is clearly distinguishable, although it laid the basis for all the later civilizations.

The iconography of Olmec art is most unusual. There are numerous figures in the form of cat or jaguar men. The figures are sexless and usually appear infantile. They are the prototype of the Rain God of the Classic period. The Olmecs excelled at sculpture, both bas-reliefs and in the round. Their works range from giant stone heads to minute figures in serpentine or jade. Pottery was also produced in the same style, both vessels and figures. Throughout their art, the jaguar plays an important part.

Perhaps the most important site of Olmec culture is La Venta, Tabasco. On an island of about two square miles, in a coastal swamp, it is eighteen miles inland from the gulf near the Tonala River. Another site of importance is Tres Zapotes about one hundred miles to the north-west. It was here that the oldest dated monument was found, a stela engraved with an abstract jaguar mask on one side, and the date 31 B.C. in the 'Long Count' calendar system on the reverse.

The birth of urban development in the second to fourth centuries marks the growth of the city of Teotihuacan and the culture named after it. Teotihuacan is the most archaeologically important city in Mexico; some estimates put its population during the Classic period at 25,000 people. Its great pyramids of the Sun and Moon and the Avenue of the Dead are amongst the wonders of Ancient America. The pyramid of the Sun is approximately two hundred feet high (61 m), with sides seven hundred feet long (213 m), while the Pyramid of the Moon is smaller, but of similar design. The architecture of the Teotihuacanos was superb; this can be seen clearly in the many ruins that have been found in the city. Beautiful painted frescoes often adorn the walls of their palaces, the most famous of which is at the Tepantitla area of the city. Here an entire wall is decorated with a painting in yellow, brown, blue and red of the Paradise of the Rain God.

Many of the superb antiquities have come from graves which are often underneath floors of buildings. Beautiful pottery vases, textiles and artefacts of obsidian normally surround the cremated remains. The typical pottery vessels of the Teotihuacanos were cylindrical and were set on tripod feet; they are often decorated in slab relief, with the recesses coloured with vermilion. Other vessels were painted in polychrome with added moulded decoration, while others are often anthropomorphic or zoomorphic in form.

The absence of the wheel in ancient America is clearly reflected in the pottery of most cultures. Unlike the symmetrical wheel-turned shapes of the ancient cultures of the western hemisphere, the shapes of Meso America are many and varied, made either by coiling or moulding. The overall art style of the Teotihuacanos is extremely sophisticated and elegant, though in many cases highly stylised. Superb sculpture in basalt, jade, greenstone and andesite is inlaid with shells and other stones.

The influence of the Teotihuacan civilization can be seen at other sites in Meso America until about 600 A.D., when it suddenly stopped. The city was destroyed by unknown invaders and was never rebuilt.

Apart from the Teotihuacan civilization, a number of civilized cultures flourished during the Classic period, influenced in some way or other by the great city. The Great Pyramid of Cholula, on the plains of Puebla, dedicated to the god Quetzalcoatl, dates to this period. It is the largest man-made structure of ancient America covering an area of twenty-five acres (10 hectares).

Another culture with a distinctive style made its appearance during

Zapotec pottery funeral urn, probably c. 13th century. From the state of Oaxaca, Mexico.

this period on the Gulf Coast Plain. This Classic Veracruz style, as it is called, is unusual and cannot be confused with any other of ancient Mexico. Its affinities lie not in America, but in China, though this similarity is only superficial. Many unusual sculptures have been found which appear to have been used in some part of an ancient ritual ball game. Classic Veracruz is sometimes called by the tribal name, Totonac, after the tribe who now occupy the region, though we have no evidence to connect them with the development of the culture. The most important site, El Tajin, lies in the rich oil-producing region of north Veracruz. Here the importance of the ritual ball game, which influenced many of the sculptures, can clearly be seen, for there are no less than seven ball courts. As in many Mexican sites, the inhabitants of El Tajin seem to have been obsessed with death, human sacrifice and the ritual ball game, a queer combination. Both death and human sacrifice were also present at the ball game, where according to bas-reliefs at the ball courts the losing captain was sacrificed by the victors. Unlike Teotihuacan, El Tajin survived the transition from the Classic to Post Classic period, but was destroyed by fire, probably by the nomadic Chichimecs in the thirteenth century.

In the Oaxaca Valley at Monte Alban another civilization flourished, that of the Zapotec. The influence of Teotihuacan can be seen, though it was fortunate, isolated as it was, not to suffer from the same disaster which fell upon Teotihuacan. Numerous fine subterranean tombs have been found at the site, with fine, though in many cases hurried, painted frescoes. Some of the ceramic funerary sculptures or urns are remarkable, being made in several sections in the forms of gods and humans, though on the whole the Zapotecs were not great potters when it came to domestic vessels. Later, the Mixtecs drove the Zapotecs from some cities and even settled at Monte Alban, and one of the funerary vaults of Monte Alban has preserved fine objects of Mixtec culture. From the fourteenth century, the area was firmly under Mixtec control.

Meso America—Maya, Toltec and Aztec

In spite of the archaeological research that has been carried out over the last hundred years, we know very little about the Maya, who occupied an area of southern Mexico, Honduras, Guatemala, and El Salvador. Looking at the remains of this great civilization it is often difficult to believe that they did not have the use of the wheel, or metals, and yet their superb buildings and sculpture testify to their brilliance as architects, artists and craftsmen. We also know that they were brilliant

Calcite vase with jaguar handles of the Mayan 'Classic' period, from the Ulua Valley region, Honduras.

astronomers and mathematicians, and their measurements of movements of heavenly bodies without the aid of any instruments has baffled modern-day astronomers. They were also literate, having developed a most elaborate hieroglyphic script. They were all these and yet they were in the Neolithic state, probably the most advanced Neolithic culture the world has seen. Some archaeologists have likened them to the Greeks of ancient Europe.

The remains of this puzzling civilization have been unearthed at a number of sites by archaeologists who have devoted their lives to un-

154

ravelling the mysteries of the Maya. Mysteries they certainly are, for around 300 B.C. there suddenly appeared, without previous evidence of development, an almost fully fledged culture which was to flourish for centuries.

Great cities grew up, capitals of city states. These, unlike many of the cities of Meso America, do not appear to have been fortified. This, and the fact that so few weapons have been found, suggests that, like the Greeks, the Maya were more interested in obscure abstract philosophy, mathematics and astronomy, than warlike pursuits. However, recent discoveries throw doubt that this was always the case. A site called Bonampak, in the state of Chiapas was discovered in 1946, which has preserved murals showing among other subjects battle scenes. The dramatic paintings which were executed in about the eighth century also show prisoners being tortured, a side of the Maya character not evident in the carved reliefs.

The Maya architects did not know the use of the arch, but roofed many of the rooms in the massive buildings with corbelling. This resulted in extremely thick walls and narrow rooms, and it is unlikely that these massive 'palaces' were lived in.

The artisans and craftsmen were extremely skilled, producing fine pottery, stone carvings, sculpture, both stelae and reliefs, and many other objects of great beauty.

At the city of Palenque, in south east Mexico, superb frescoes and a massive stone slab were found in the centre of the largest pyramid. Archaeologists examining the floor of the temple on the pyramid noticed that one of the floor stones was larger than the others. It was raised and, much to their surprise, they found an entrance stairway leading into the interior of the pyramid, but they could not enter as it was blocked by rubble. In 1952 this was excavated. The stairway led to a massive stone door, which, when displaced, revealed a large chamber. On the walls were larger than life-size paintings of priests and in the centre of the room was a large stone slab resting on a rectangular block of stone. The slab, which was covered with the most exquisite relief carvings, was raised to reveal the skeleton of the priest-king to whom the pyramid had been dedicated. It is the only pyramid so far found in America that was constructed specifically as a tomb, a fact often forgotten by those who seek to connect the Egyptian civilization with that of ancient America. Apart from the geographical separation, there is a long interval of some three thousand years between the erection of the structures which also differ architecturally. In spite of this,

Excavation of the Temple of the Sun and the Palace at Palenque, Chiapas, Mexico.

there have been pseudo-academic attempts to connect Egyptian and American cultures. The recent success of the papyrus boat 'Ra' only proves that papyrus boats were seaworthy, with luck, and that it was possible to cross the ocean, but it does not prove in any way that this was actually done.

The classic period of the Maya lasted from about the third century A.D. for some six hundred years. The end of the Maya cities is almost as puzzling as the beginning. The cities were simply abandoned gradually, the inhabitants moving elsewhere, many to the Yucatan Peninsula, and the cities of Uxmal and Chichen Itza. By the tenth century, all their old territory had been abandoned. Today there are still some descendants of the Maya such as the primitive tribe, the Lacondones, who still live in the old Maya territory.

The Toltecs had arrived in Yucatan, from the north, towards the end of the tenth century, and had taken over the city of Chichen Itza. Although the Maya buildings of the city are still standing it is the imposing Toltec architecture which attracts our attention today. The Toltec influence can be clearly seen in such monuments as the famous Temple of Warriors. They transformed Chichen Itza into a new version of their home capital of Tula, north of the Valley of Mexico. The most famous of ancient American sculptural forms, the reclining figure of Chac-Mool, was introduced into Chichen Itza by the Toltecs.

While the Maya gods were placated by the self sacrifices and mutilations of the devotees, the Toltec gods were more demanding, requiring a constant supply of human sacrifices. In order to keep the priests supplied, they had to wage continual war to obtain suitable victims. Chichen Itza lost its political power in 1200 A.D. to the city state of Mayapan, which held power over Yucatan for a period of some two hundred and fifty years. Under its strong military government, the arts declined. Pottery became mass-produced from moulds, with little individuality.

If the Maya were the Greeks of ancient America, the Aztecs were the Romans. They originated as a small tribe of not more than a thousand, living on a few islands on Lake Texaco, but their ruthless determination, organisation and commercial enterprise resulted in their dominating a substantial part of Mexico. They extracted taxes from their subject tribes over a vast area. Warring tribes had forced the Toltecs to move southward, abandoning their city of Tula in 1168. These warring tribes followed southward, the last of whom were the Aztecs who settled in the valley of Mexico. Although we call them the Aztecs after their homeland of Aztlan, by the time they had settled in the valley they were calling themselves Mexica. They seized the opportunity of the inter-city warfare being waged in the valley to establish themselves as a military and political power.

One of the first identifiable historical personages of ancient Mexico was their leader, Nezahualcoyotl, a man of remarkable talent, both as a statesman and civil engineer. He built an aqueduct, carrying drinking water across Lake Texaco to the city of Tenochtitlan, that remained in use after the Spanish conquest, until the water supply dried up. Nezahualcoyotl died in 1472. The Aztecs were great architects, but above all they were great organisers, and utilised the skills of their subject peoples to great effect.

As we have said, the Spanish marvelled at what they saw, and although they destroyed much, they also took back objects to Europe, some of which have survived to the present day and are in museums. Archaeology has given us objects, while early written accounts describe yet others. The first 'exhibition' of Mexican art was held in Brussels in 1520. It fascinated Europeans, and the German artist, Durer, who was in the city at the time, described with astonishment what he saw. He described weapons, armour, clothing and objects in gold, silver and stones: 'I have never seen anything that gave me such delight as did these objects'. Today it is probably the monstrous aspect of Aztec art evident in sculpture, painting and pottery, that attracts us most. The shapes appear extremely modern, exercising a primitive cubism. Most works were not, however, executed as art but as accessories to their barbaric religion, a religion that required the wholesale sacrifice of human beings, and indeed most of their art centred around this tendency. On one occasion between twenty thousand and one hundred thousand human sacrifices were made to consecrate a new temple. This repelled the Spanish Conquistadors as much as they were attracted by the material aspects of their culture.

The Aztecs believed that the end of the world would occur at the end of their fifty-two year calendar cycle, and in preparation for this they destroyed their possessions. A number of caches have been found by archaeologists and we have been able to evolve a system of dating the pottery into four periods of fifty-two years. It is now possible to trace the evolution of Aztec ceramic painting back to 1299.

The numerous cultures of ancient America are just beginning to be understood and we can be sure that in the future many more fascinating discoveries will be made.

Peru

The great South American civilizations of Peru have left a wealth of material remains, as great as any in Meso America. Unfortunately, the antiquities are so prolific that they have been the target of treasure hunters rather than archaeologists. It would be untrue, however, to say that this was the only source of antiquities of their cultures, for archaeological excavations have taken place and it is to these that we owe much of our knowledge.

As with Meso America, there were early primitive cultures, but the civilizations which concern us most today are those of the Chimu, Chancay, Nazca and Incas. There were others, including those of the Paracas and the Chavin and here there seem to be some affinities with the Olmec style of Meso America. There are also the Recauy and the Moche.

The Moche culture flourished in a few valleys of northern Peru. Its ceramic ware, though influenced by earlier cultures, is distinctive and it made the first ceramic portrait head vessels. One of the largest of ancient Peruvian monuments, the stepped pyramid which the Spanish called 'the Sanctuary of the Sun', was made during the advanced state of culture. We know very little about the culture, except that which can be gleaned from the scenes on painted pottery vessels. Most of the remains have come from the burrowing of treasure hunters and not archaeological excavations. We know from the painted scenes that the Moche people were warriors and indulged in battles, seemingly with themselves as well as with others. We also know that, like the peoples of Meso America, they practised human sacrifice. Scenes of everyday life show hunting parties, fishing and weaving and the dead and even erotic scenes are also depicted.

We know even less about the Nazca culture than we do of the Moche people. The culture developed almost simultaneously with the Moche, but although we have a wealth of Nazca pottery vessels, they are not decorated with the same informative scenes as the Moche. Dates are rare in Peruvian archaeology, and it is difficult to establish more than relative chronologies, and although radiocarbon dating is coming to our aid, what is really needed is more scientific excavation. With the Nazca culture we are a little more fortunate as we know there was a proto-Nazca period, extending roughly from the fourth century A.D. to the fifth century; Middle Nazca extended from approximately the fourth century A.D. to the sixth century (here there is an overlap); and thereafter Late Nazca continued until after 1000 A.D.

The polychrome ware of the Nazcas is amongst the most beautiful in South America. The colour range is superb, with different shades and tints, and the painting is usually on a white or red ground. Most vessels have a fine burnished surface which give the pots a glazed appearance. The shapes are varied and distinctive, being formed mainly by coiling though moulding was used to a certain extent. Subjects too are numerous. Another great aspect of Nazca art was their textiles, which emulated the colour schemes of the pottery.

Another culture, though not in modern Peru, but an important part of the cultural heritage of ancient Peru, is the Tiahuanaco, named after a village in Bolivia. The Tiahuanaco pottery is superbly coloured in polychrome. Their sculptors were experts both in colossal as well as miniature carvings and clay sculpture was also made, reminiscent of the sculptures in stone. Mythological figures were common. Dates again are difficult; however, there is one radiocarbon date which places the classic Tiahuanaco period to about 500 A.D., but this may be quite unreliable— we simply do not know. Here again there have been few scientific excavations to help, sometimes through governmental restrictions, though also through lack of interest. In about the ninth century A.D. the Tiahuanaco began to make itself felt in other areas.

Before the Incas, between the fourteenth and fifteenth centuries, there was a period of minor principalities, amongst them the Chimu. Chimu influence was felt over a large area of Peru, from the northern Moche valley southward to Lima. Another principality was that of the Cuismanca, which controlled the valley of the River Chancay to the Rimac Valley; and there were others, including the Aymora and the Cajamarca of the northern sierra, who allied themselves with the Chimu to defend themselves from the Incas. The Chimu princes lived at Chanchan, a well-planned city, which has been a Mecca for the treasure hunter for years, though here again no large scale archaeological excavations have taken place. The black pottery vessels of the Chimu have been found in a wide area of Peru.

The Incas, as a term for a people, is actually incorrect, for it was a term applied to the head of the Quechua Indians. The Inca was also the representation of the Sun on earth, and as such worshipped in temples. Through their expansionist policy of conquest, the Quechua dominated a vast area from Ecuador to northern Chile. Under their rule, the country prospered and the arts flourished. It was perhaps the flower of Peruvian culture. Originally, under Pachacutec (1438–71) their territory was small. Later, under Tupac Yupawqui (1471–93), the period of their main expansion took place with just a few areas in the north being added under Huayana Copac (1493–1525).

The Incas were unable to write, their only form of written communication being the Quipu or knotted cord, by which even complicated historical thoughts could be recorded. The first history of the Inca empire was written shortly after the Spanish conquest, by the Cieza de Leon. We are most fortunate that he was able to record the history of the empire, which had been passed on by word of mouth.

Not all the Inca conquests were made by force of arms; some were the result of high pressure diplomacy. Once subjugated, the conquered had to embrace the religion of the Sun, becoming part of the empire of the Sun, although they were also allowed to keep their own local deities.

The Quechua were great architects and builders. They did not decorate the interiors of their buildings with frescoes, but preferred to decorate them with tapestries. Gold was the cause of their downfall for their use of the metal attracted the Spanish, who overran them and destroyed Indian civilization in the southern continent of America forever. Today, however, we have little Inca gold work and what we do have comes from graves or chance finds. The Spanish shipped back to Spain shiploads of golden objects, but not one has survived as they were all melted down.

The archaeology of the Americas is just emerging, the period of treasure hunting we hope has passed, and we can look forward to new discoveries, by future generations of archaeologists, to fill in our meagre knowledge of these cultures.

Index

The figures in bold refer to colour plates. Those in italics refer to the page numbers of black and white illustrations. Other figures refer to text pages.

165

167